Heading l
Wether
and
Dreams of Leaving

HEADING HOME

Wetherby and
Dreams of Leaving

David Hare

faber and faber
LONDON · BOSTON

First published in 1991
by Faber and Faber Limited
3 Queen Square London WC1N 3AU

Photoset by Parker Typesetting Service Leicester
Printed in Great Britain by Clays Ltd St Ives plc

David Hare is hereby identified as author of this work in accordance with section 77 of the Copyright, Design and Patents Act 1988.

Wetherby was first published by Faber and Faber in association with Greenpoint Films Ltd in 1985; *Dreams of Leaving* was first published by Faber and Faber in 1980.

The quotation from 'In Memory of W. B. Yeats' by W. H. Auden is from *The English Auden* edited by Edward Mendelson, reprinted by permission of Faber and Faber Limited.

A CIP record for this book is available from the British Library

ISBN 0-571-16244 4

In memory
Alan Clarke

Contents

HEADING HOME

———

'Wars are like weddings: essentially extravagant and unnecessary, but a great stimulant in a convention-bound society.'

Arthur Marwick

Heading Home was first shown on BBC2 in January 1991. The cast included:

JANETTA WHEATLAND	Joely Richardson
LEONARD MEOPHAM	Stephen Dillane
BERYL JAMES	Stella Gonet
MR EVERNDEN	John Moffatt
MR ASHCROFT	Leon Eagles
LESLEY PEROWNE	Sandy McDade
IAN TYSON	Gary Oldman
JULIUSZ JANOWSKI	Eugene Lipinski
MRS GILL	Lollie May
CHAMBERMAID	Lesley Mackie
ROMAN	Alan Pattison
OLD WOMAN	Ruth Kettlewell
AUCTIONEER	Doyne Bird
STAMFORD HILL COWBOY	David Schneider
DEREK GREEN	Michael Bryant
CHARLIE	Julian Firth
ANTON	Paul Reeves
Director	David Hare
Producer	Rick McCallum
Photography	Oliver Stapleton
Design	Derek Dodd
Music	Stanley Myers
Costume	Hazel Pethig
Executive Producer	Mark Shivas

I. CREDITS. DAY

A young woman is running along a beach. She is twenty-three. It is
JANETTA. *Her hair is blowing in the wind. The background is clear*
behind her until we fade up under her through a series of dissolves:
images of flowing water, railway wires, shelves of books. The size of
her image also changes through dissolves as the words 'Heading Home'
arrive. Music plays, lyrical and English underneath. We see her, still
running, in profile as the background dissolves again and is replaced
by a pattern of leaves with sun blazing through them. When her image
fades, we are left simply with a subjective camera looking up to sun
through the trees, a pure pattern of green and gold. Then coming
through the music, the sound of JANETTA*'s voice.*

JANETTA: (*Voice over*) That route to the beach, I can only tell you,
　　　it always seemed special. That particular road was quite
　　　extraordinary, even at the time.
　　　(*Now with the subjective camera again as if from a moving*
　　　vehicle, we see an English country lane seeming to career towards
　　　us, the sun still flashing in our eyes.)
　　　There were trees either side for – what? – maybe a mile.
　　　Then the road opened out quite suddenly.
　　　(*The road suddenly seems to widen and open out as we reach a*
　　　beach.)
　　　You saw the beach and the bay.

2. EXT. BEACH. DAY

On the beach. A stretch of sand, and dunes beyond with tufts of grass
among them, the camera moving round, close to the waterside, as if
held by an unseen hand. Into the shot, laughing, circling, in the
manner of a snapshot, comes JANETTA. *It is 1947. She is wearing a*
full bathing costume, dark with crossed straps around the neck. She is
laughing at a MAN *we do not see.*

JANETTA: (*Voice over*) Even then it was quite different from
　　　anywhere else.
　　　(*There is a voice from behind the camera.*)
LEONARD: (*Out of shot*) Come over here.
JANETTA: I'm not coming. I know what you want.

LEONARD: (*Out of shot*) Then come over.

(*She stops a moment, shy, the head sideways, the eyes down, in the way of the young. And then slowly she begins to walk towards the camera, her mood entirely changed.*)

3. EXT. THE DUNES. DAY

JANETTA *lying on her back in the dunes*, LEONARD *coming into frame to kiss her, his hand indside her costume. They are both dark-haired, hers in a perm behind her, his thick and curly. He is short, about six years older than her. They kiss and laugh in the sun, the grass and sand behind them.*

Then the camera lifts from the dunes to show how well they are hidden from the fifteen other people who are scattered about on the sands. A couple of families, the children playing; some ramblers who have sat down to rest in the sun; prominently, some picnickers eating from cloths on the sand.

There is space for everyone in the bay, great distances between them all. Perfect contentment.

JANETTA: (*Voice over*) It never seemed like England. When you think of English beaches, you think of pebbles. And this one always had sand.

4. INT. PUB. NIGHT

Winter 1946/7. A packed pub in North Soho. Mahogany and glass. Everyone wrapped in overcoats and scarves, even indoors. Light bulbs, thick smoke, nearly everyone drinking beer. It is ferociously busy, with no room to stand anywhere, but JANETTA *is sitting in a big blue overcoat at a table against the wall next to* BERYL, *a woman in her mid-twenties who is wearing a huge, rather old, fur coat. Behind them the wall is decked out with photographs. In front of them, a number of empty bottles and a seat which is empty.*

BERYL *is talking animatedly, then makes a joke and laughs, while* JANETTA *sits, young, attentive beside her.*

JANETTA: (*Voice over*) I'm racing ahead. I know I shouldn't. I'll start somewhere else . . .

(LEONARD *is at the bar where there is a fight to get served in the crush of people. In everything he does there is an economy of gestures, a precision which speaks of a confidence that people will*

6

come to him. A cigarette hangs from his mouth, his overcoat and scarf are wrapped neatly around him. He carries some bottles through the crowd above his head.)

I'll start when I'd just met Leonard. And I was in London for the first time.

(LEONARD *forces his way through to the table.*)

LEONARD: It's so bloody cold, you've got to have another.

JANETTA: I don't want another.

BERYL: She hasn't had a first.

(LEONARD *sits down beside them.*)

JANETTA: I don't even drink.

BERYL: She will.

JANETTA: Yes, I know.

BERYL: It's the only way to keep warm.

(*They smile a moment.* BERYL *looks between them.*)

So you met today?

JANETTA: Yes.

BERYL: How?

JANETTA: Accidentally.

LEONARD: Sort of.

(JANETTA *smiles, a little nervous.*)

JANETTA: I wrote a letter.

LEONARD: It wasn't to me.

JANETTA: No.

LEONARD: It was to Charlie.

BERYL: Who's Charlie?

LEONARD: He's another poet.

(LEONARD'*s voice is suddenly quite dry.*)

JANETTA: I heard him on the wireless. I liked his voice. So he wrote back saying come into the studio, and as I was in London and I hardly know anyone, I thought, why not?
(*She smiles, a little unsure of her own courage.*)
Only somehow, I don't know, I arrived to see Charlie, and I left with Leonard.

(BERYL *looks at* LEONARD, *who is expressionless.*)

I can't quite work it out.

(BERYL *smiles contentedly.*)

BERYL: Well, you don't seem unhappy.

JANETTA: No. Leonard showed me the studio. That sort of thing.

(JANETTA *frowns for a moment, hesitant to go on.*)

7

Do you . . .

LEONARD: What?

JANETTA: Do you drink here every evening?

LEONARD: There's a group of us, yes.

BERYL: All the riff-raff.

(LEONARD *smiles*.)

LEONARD: Beryl's a sculptor.

BERYL: Was a sculptor. Until I had a baby. So now I have to work
with one hand.

(*She mimes holding a baby in one arm and hammering with the
other.*)

JANETTA: Have you left him at home?

BERYL: I don't have a home. I'm staying at friends' houses.
That's another problem.

JANETTA: Does he have a father?

(BERYL *looks at her, not unkindly, just assessing her youth.*)

BERYL: Why, no.

(JANETTA *frowns, not understanding, then looks to* LEONARD,
who just smiles.)

JANETTA: I don't understand. Where is he?

BERYL: It's all right. He's in the warm.

5. INT. PASSAGEWAY. NIGHT

*The passageway at the back of the pub, which leads to a staircase and
the private rooms. It is where all the drink is stored. At the end of the
corridor there is a door open to the pub, a square of light with smoke
and people chattering. Right by the stairs, there is a pile of beer crates.*
JANETTA *is standing immediately behind* BERYL, *as* BERYL *leans
down towards the top crate. Inside, a baby,* SAM, *is fast asleep,
serene, tucked up warm in his covers.* BERYL *lifts* SAM *out.*

BERYL: Come on little fellow. There, there. That's a good little
fellow. Yes, yes.

(*She lifts him up and smiles at him, then drops him inside her
capacious coat.*)

Come on.

(*She closes the flap of her coat over him. His face disappears
inside the coat.*)

Let's face the cold.

6. EXT. STREET. NIGHT

They fight their way along the street in the snow.

We are quite close so they are just a huddled group in the night, snow blowing across their faces, but the street and pavement are indistinct behind them, and nothing else moves in the background.

LEONARD: Everyone knows there aren't any readers.

JANETTA: No readers?

LEONARD: Everyone's given up reading books. Since the war.

JANETTA: Why is that?

LEONARD: The only reason people read was because of the
blackout. They had to stay in. There was nothing else to do.
(*He turns a moment and looks at her.* BERYL *has hurried on out
of sight, sheltering* SAM *against the snow.*)
It meant people read. But now the war's over.
(*And he too has disappeared, leaving* JANETTA *last to turn,
alone.*)

JANETTA: Yes, I can see. I can see that's a bore.

7. INT. LEONARD'S ROOM. NIGHT

*They come into Leonard's flat, shaking the snow off their boots as they
enter.*

*He lives in a single room, high above Bloomsbury. The walls are
brown and there is little decoration save for some improvised
bookshelves. There is a cheerless gas fire.*

In one corner is a bed and in the other a table at which LEONARD
plainly works and eats.

*The effect is orderly – that of a man forced to be economic with
space.*

Now LEONARD *has stooped to put some coins in the gas meter.*

BERYL *has parked* SAM *on Leonard's bed and is taking a mattress
from a cupboard and laying it on the floor with the air of someone well
practised in this particular routine.*

This leaves JANETTA, *still in her coat, standing rather lost in the
centre of the room.*

LEONARD: Will you sleep here?

JANETTA: Oh.
(*She stops, not knowing what to say.* BERYL *is putting blankets
on the mattress.*)

Well, I hadn't thought to.

BERYL: I am. So's Sam. Leonard's one of my very kind friends.

(LEONARD *returns.* BERYL *kisses* LEONARD's *cheek, in passing.* JANETTA *watches.*)

Thank you, dear.

(*They kiss.*)

LEONARD: Not at all. (*He turns to* JANETTA.) Well?

JANETTA: I'd like to. It's just my aunt is expecting me.

LEONARD: Why don't you telephone? There's one on the landing. Tell her the buses can't get through the snow.

(JANETTA *hesitates.*)

Why not? No harm can come to you. It'll save you a very nasty journey. And it's no trouble to us.

(JANETTA *smiles.*)

JANETTA: All right.

(LEONARD *is now gathering up some books from around the room and putting them on the table.* BERYL *is putting* SAM *into the little bed she has made, ignoring them both, just getting on with it.*)

LEONARD: I'm going to write. It shouldn't disturb you. I'll just use a very low light.

JANETTA: Good.

LEONARD: You sleep there.

(*He points to his own bed.*)

JANETTA: Fine.

LEONARD: Beside Beryl.

(JANETTA *frowns again.* BERYL *has got into her bed, without taking her fur coat off, next to the sleeping* SAM.)

JANETTA: Where will you sleep?

LEONARD: Oh, I'll work through the night. I'll be fine. (*He smiles at her, suddenly quiet.*) Then when you get up, I'll go to bed.

(*Just as he is about to turn away, we hear* JANETTA's *voice.*)

JANETTA: (*Voice over*) I don't know, I'd never met anyone like him . . .

8. INT. MONTAGE

Voice over continuous. Montage of images from later that night in the flat. First, JANETTA *lying in the bed, her eyes open. Then her point of view of* BERYL *and* SAM *fast asleep below her on their mattress, side by side.*

JANETTA: (*Voice over*) In fact I'd never slept a night away from
my family. I lay there, I watched Leonard for a while . . .
(JANETTA's *point of view of* LEONARD's *back. He is sitting in
the chair at the desk; only the lamp is on. He is hunched over his
writing.*)
I liked the arch of his back. I liked his hand moving across
the paper.
(LEONARD *leans in slightly towards his work.*)
And then I slept like a top.

9. INT. LIBRARY. DAY

*The conference room of a large Victorian private library. Gothic
bookcases, glass-fronted, with a large table suitable for committee
meetings and high-backed leather chairs. Framed documents and
photographs on the wall.* MR EVERNDEN *is in his fifties, in a thick
suit with a blue and grey stripe. He is elaborately donnish in his
manner.* MR ASHCROFT, *the senior librarian, sits in thick brown
tweed, thunder-browed, in his mid-sixties, largely letting* EVERNDEN
get on with it. JANETTA *is smartly dressed, opposite.*

EVERNDEN: What is your background?

JANETTA: Oh, I don't have any.

ASHCROFT: No background?

JANETTA: Oh, in libraries, I mean. Of course I have a
background. (*She smiles nervously.*) I was brought up in
Somerset.

EVERNDEN: Do you have any qualifications?

JANETTA: I don't.
(*There is a slight pause, so she fills in.*)
My father kept a shop.

EVERNDEN: For instance, did you go to school?

JANETTA: Yes, but they only taught us manners.

EVERNDEN: I see. (*He smiles slightly, liking her.*) Well, as long as
you intend to spend a lifetime in libraries . . .

JANETTA: Oh yes, may I?
(*This comes out a little overly enthusiastic, so she looks down and
moderates her tone to fit the subdued atmosphere.*)
I mean, that's very kind.

10. INT. STACKS. DAY

The open stacks of the library. Row upon row of books, in metal grille-work stretching up floor after floor. In the thin corridor between the stacks, JANETTA *is standing, being shown the ropes by* LESLEY, *a strikingly tall, thin girl with a long nose, in her mid-twenties.*

LESLEY: This is science and miscellaneous. For instance . . . (*She points to various shelves.*) Nature. Natural disasters. Natural history.

JANETTA: Ah yes.

LESLEY: It's all arranged according to subject. All we do is stick stuff back on the shelf. You'll get used to it.
   (JANETTA *nods, taking this in.*)

JANETTA: And how do we decide what category a book is?
   (LESLEY *doesn't even turn towards her.*)

LESLEY: Oh, that's not up to us. That's done by people with brains.

11. INT. CORRIDOR. EVENING

JANETTA *sitting alone in the corridor outside the studios at the BBC. The corridor is cream and shabby-carpeted like the lower-deck passageways in a big ocean liner. At once the studio door opens, and* LEONARD *comes out, in a suit, expecting to go home.* JANETTA, *in a suit, stands up. He's surprised to see her.*

LEONARD: My goodness, it's you.

JANETTA: Yes. I thought I'd wait for you. Do you mind?
(LEONARD *smiles.*)

LEONARD: I never mind anything.

(*As the door closes behind him we just glimpse the studio with a couple of producers winding up work.*)

JANETTA: I just got a job and I wanted to celebrate. So the best way seemed to be to come and tell you.

LEONARD: Well done. Where's the job?

JANETTA: In a library.

LEONARD: In a library? Why?
   (*She smiles, turning away, embarrassed, finding the courage to go on.*)

JANETTA: I don't know, it's silly. Last night your hand . . .

LEONARD: My hand?

JANETTA: Yes. I was lying there watching, last night, as you
wrote, you were writing, I couldn't help it, I just thought:
I'd like this life. And so it's time I learnt one or two things
about things.

LEONARD: Yes.

JANETTA: I'll work in a library. (*She looks down a moment.*) Also,
another thing, I've decided not to go back to my aunt's.
(*He just looks at her.*)
Because I know she's going to be angry. I thought this
morning, why put myself through all that? I thought perhaps
if I moved out for ever, then that's *that* problem out of the
way.
(*He is still looking at her, giving nothing away.*)
Do you think that's wrong? Am I being crazy?

LEONARD: It depends. Do you have somewhere to go?
(*There's a pause. She looks at him.*)

JANETTA: It wouldn't be for long. Just while I'm looking. Would
you mind? Would you mind terribly?
(*His expression doesn't change.*)

LEONARD: I'd say if I did.

12. INT. PUB. NIGHT

*The pub crammed again. Now the table at which they sat last night is
crowded with* LEONARD's *friends – writers, artists, old Soho men and
women, regular drinkers, all wrapped in coats and scarves.* JANETTA
*is at the centre of the group, a glass of beer in front of her. We look
down on the group as* LEONARD *stands up, silencing the noisy,
laughing group around him to make an announcement.*

LEONARD: All right, quiet please, quiet please, everyone.
(*There is silence.*)
Janetta's first glass of ale.
(*There is a moment's pause, then* JANETTA *lifts the glass to her
lips.*)

13. INT. ROOM. NIGHT

Under the lamp on Leonard's table JANETTA *is holding photographs
of her family. First we see a picture of a thickset man in his mid-
sixties, standing outside a large haberdasher's. The store, which is four*

windows wide, has its awnings down, and a hand-painted shop sign reading 'Wheatlands'. The man is looking self-consciously to the camera, the pole for lowering the awnings in his hand.

JANETTA: This is the shop.

LEONARD: Uh-huh.

JANETTA: Ridiculous. I know. This is Mummy.

(*A surprisingly large woman, in a floral dress, as if going to church, in her fifties, also standing outside the same shop. Then at once JANETTA's hand shows us a group of six girls who are all walking down the middle of the road in what is obviously a respectable middle-sized town. They are all holding each other round the waist, and roaring with laughter. They range in age from their mid-thirties to about sixteen. JANETTA is the penultimate. All of them are in summer dresses.*)

My sisters.

LEONARD: Gracious.

JANETTA: I'm one of six.

LEONARD: Well, well.

JANETTA: I know.

(*And now, for the first time, we see the context. LEONARD and JANETTA are sitting close by one another on the table, their knees in front of them, their feet on chairs. After LEONARD has seen each photo he hands it on to BERYL, who stands slightly to one side.*)

Mummy said, go to London, learn shorthand typing so you can help Dad with the paperwork until . . .

(*She stops.*)

LEONARD: Until what?

JANETTA: Well, obviously until I get married.

(*BERYL is looking at the picture of the six girls, and her tone is much more serious than the other two's.*)

BERYL: They look very nice. I don't have any family, so I think you're very lucky.

(*As she says this, she moves across and kisses JANETTA on the cheek, a little sadly. Then, saying no more, she goes across to where there are now two mattresses on the floor, one of them Janetta's, the other with SAM already asleep on it. Silently, BERYL gets into bed, still in her coat, and pulls the blankets up. There is a silence. LEONARD and JANETTA are very close, not moving, as if suddenly alone.*)

14

LEONARD: And have you told them you're going to stay here?

14. INT. LEONARD'S ROOM. NIGHT

JANETTA, *coming into the room, is about to turn the light on, when she hears a voice.*

BERYL: Hello.

> (JANETTA *looks through the near-dark and realizes that* BERYL *is lying in a tin bath in the centre of the room, stretched out, enjoying a cigarette. Only the dim light comes in from outside.*)

JANETTA: Oh, I'm sorry.

BERYL: It's fine. I was just enjoying a cigarette.

> (*Without turning the light on,* JANETTA *sits down on the bed.*)

JANETTA: I hope you don't mind my coming to stay.

> (BERYL *smiles at her, to say no.*)

Have you known Leonard long?

BERYL: He was in the Navy. He used to be in Arctic convoys. You should talk to him about it.

JANETTA: I will. (*She looks down a moment.*) I didn't . . . I hope you don't think that . . . well, I don't want to come between you . . .

BERYL: What do you mean?

JANETTA: Well, I just meant . . . I wasn't sure if you were his girlfriend or not.

BERYL: What on earth made you think that?

> (*She is lying quite still in the bath, only moving her hand to draw on her cigarette.* JANETTA *is very conscious of her nakedness in front of her.* BERYL's *tone is gentle, amused.*)

Of course not. Why? Me and Leonard?

JANETTA: No, it was silly. I got it wrong.

BERYL: Don't worry. Why did you think that?

JANETTA: I don't know. It's just . . . (*She stops a moment, then shrugs slightly.*) It's so easy between you. The way you sleep here. The way he takes it for granted you will.

BERYL: Why, yes. Because we're friends.

> (BERYL *smiles, thinking a moment.*)

And part of the fun is, things don't need saying. Isn't that what friendship is about? You don't have to say anything. And yet things are understood between you. (*She frowns a moment.*) Don't you have friends like that?

15

JANETTA: Not yet. (*She is very quiet. She looks away.*) I'd like to though.

15. INT. LIBRARY. DAY

EVERNDEN's *area of the library. It is a magnificent Victorian area, with a series of desks, catalogues and shelves.* EVERNDEN *is seated at his desk.* JANETTA *enters the room and walks to his desk.*)

JANETTA: Mr Evernden. I hope you don't mind . . .
(*He looks up.*)
You know when books are returned, they're stored alphabetically . . .

EVERNDEN: Yes.

JANETTA: Then they're taken across and they're re-sorted by subject before they're put back on the shelf . . .
(EVERNDEN *just looks at her, not reacting. She puts down the books she is carrying and leans on them.*)
But if they had been stored by subject in the first place, that would eliminate one stage of work.
(EVERNDEN *frowns.*)

EVERNDEN: But the card index is also alphabetical.

JANETTA: It could be by subject.
(LESLEY *has turned from where she is working and is surreptitiously listening to them.* EVERNDEN *hesitates, reluctant to hand her this point publicly.*)
It seems so obvious, I'm amazed no one's thought of it.
(EVERNDEN *catches* LESLEY's *eyes.*)

EVERNDEN: Miss Perowne, I'm talking to Miss Wheatland.
(LESLEY *turns away.*)
Sometimes it needs an outsider's eye.

16. INT. LIBRARY. NIGHT

An overall, high view of the library, now locked up for the night, a few lights burning as JANETTA *gathers up the final cards to replace them in their boxes, which are spread out in front of her on the floor. At the far side of the room* EVERNDEN *is working silently at his desk.* JANETTA *finishes.*

JANETTA: There you are, it's done.

EVERNDEN: I congratulate you.

16

JANETTA: I've also reclassified the shelves.
   (*She points to the shelves behind her. There are subject labels, in
   neat calligraphy.*)
   Actually I had another idea . . .
   (*But before she can speak* EVERNDEN *interrupts.*)
EVERNDEN: No, please, just leave it. At least for a week or two.
   We can only manage a single idea at a time.
   (*He smiles at her from across the enormous distance of the
   library's ground floor.*)
   You know we had a bomb . . .
JANETTA: Yes.
EVERNDEN: And yet we opened next morning. We handed out
   books in the street. (*He pauses a moment.*) Perhaps it's a fault.
   We've not thought about change. Just about survival.
   (*She watches him, equally still on her side of the room.*)
   Now here you are to shake us all up.

17. INT. LEONARD'S ROOM. NIGHT

At once LEONARD *working, undisturbed, at his desk. The room is
empty but for him. Then the door opens and* JANETTA *comes in,
exhausted, breathless.*
JANETTA: Oh goodness, I'm so late.
LEONARD: It's all right.
   (*He turns and smiles at her. She has stopped where she is, and is
   looking round. There is no sign of anyone else. There is only one
   mattress on the floor, and* BERYL *and* SAM *have gone, all trace of
   them.*)
JANETTA: Where's Sam? Where's Beryl?
LEONARD: She came in and said she'd been offered another place.
JANETTA: Well, gracious.
   (LEONARD *is quite steady and quiet, looking at her, not raising
   his voice, just level.*)
LEONARD: She said you and I might like to be alone.
   (JANETTA *looks at him, but before she can speak, he turns back
   to his work, so she can't.*)
   I'm going to work.
JANETTA: Uh-huh.
   (JANETTA *stands a moment, left by herself. He has started
   writing again. She sits down on the edge of the bed and reaches*

17

into her pocket. *She gets out a large hunk of pork pie, which she unwraps from its greaseproof paper. It looks pretty solid. She picks at it for a moment.*)

Do you want a piece of pie?

LEONARD: No, thank you.

(*She looks at it, not moving. Then she puts it aside.*)

JANETTA: I think I should be going to bed.

18. INT. LEONARD'S ROOM. NIGHT

Later. JANETTA *is in the little kitchen area stirring milk into a cup of cocoa. She is thickly wrapped in at least two pairs of pyjamas, and a dressing gown, with an extra sweater. As she stirs the cocoa she turns and takes a look at* LEONARD, *but he is characteristically bent over his desk, not looking at her.*

JANETTA: (*Voice over*) It would happen. We both knew it would happen. In a way it was like the phoney war . . .

19. INT. LEONARD'S ROOM. NIGHT

Later. JANETTA *is lying in bed as* LEONARD *turns off the light at his desk then walks by her, his pyjamaed legs just a couple of feet away from her bed.*

JANETTA: (*Voice over*) And it was delicious. Waiting. And knowing. And neither of us making a move.

20. INT. LIBRARY. DAY

At once, a book is thrown down rudely on the counter at the library, like an old can, discarded, finished with.

JANETTA *behind the desk, looks up sharply.*

Opposite her is a man in his early thirties, with a thick, pale face, gleaming slightly, like a bull toad. He is wearing a huge coat. He has a slight smile on his face. His name is IAN TYSON.

Behind him, looking the other way, as if bored to have entered a library, is a man a few years younger, very thickset and bulky, in an even larger, darker brown coat. He speaks with a thick Polish accent. His name is JULIUSZ JANOWSKI.

JANETTA: What's this?

IAN: It's a book. (*He smiles.*) You're new here.

JANETTA: Can I have your name?

IAN: It looks to me like you're too good for this place.

(IAN *has leant over the counter and is looking* JANETTA *straight in the eye.* JULIUSZ *is restless behind him, obviously bored with* IAN's *manner with girls.*)

JULIUSZ: Come on, Ian. What you doing?

(IAN *takes no notice of him*).

IAN: You don't look like the others. Well, do you?

(JANETTA *looks at him a moment. Behind her, a couple of etiolated young men are working. They do look quite bookish.*)

JANETTA: I'm sorry. I'm afraid I don't know what you mean.

(IAN *smiles, as if he doesn't believe her.*)

IAN: You don't have a defect. You're not four foot five. You don't have a hunchback. It doesn't look as if you're lame. You don't belong in a library. You look like once you got outside, you might actually be a normal person.

(JULIUSZ *is getting restless behind* IAN.)

JULIUSZ: Ian, we haven't got time for this.

(EVERNDEN *has arrived behind the desk, having seen these two strange men arrive from behind the reception area. He seems uncharacteristically harassed.*)

EVERNDEN: Miss Wheatland, I'll deal with this.

(IAN *just smiles conspiratorially at* JANETTA.)

JULIUSZ: Hello, Mr Evernden, you're looking well.

EVERNDEN: Well, thank you.

(EVERNDEN *looks between them.*)

How can we help you?

JULIUSZ: Oh, we're fine, aren't we, Ian?

(*But* IAN *just smiles at* JANETTA, *as if at some unheard joke.* IAN *hands* JANETTA *the book.*)

IAN: I'm here to give a book back.

JANETTA: (*Taking the book*) Name, please?

EVERNDEN: His name is Mr Tyson.

JANETTA: Thank you.

(*And suddenly* TYSON *winks at* JANETTA *and turns, without saying anything more and walks out of the library.* JULIUSZ *follows him, equally silent.* EVERNDEN *stands a moment, watching them go.*)

Goodness. Who was he? It doesn't look like he reads.

EVERNDEN: Oh, he reads

(JANETTA *frowns, catching* EVERNDEN's *unusually sharp tone.*
Then she looks at the book.)

JANETTA: It's a property survey.

(EVERNDEN *looks at her a moment, then turns away.*)

It's a history of Notting Hill.

(JANETTA *is thoughtful as* EVERNDEN *disappears.*)

JANETTA: (*Voice over*) The germ was there. I'd met Ian Tyson . . .

21. INT. LEONARD'S ROOM. NIGHT

We see LEONARD, *sitting working characteristically at his desk, close*
on his hand moving across the paper.

   JANETTA's *hand appears as she places it over* LEONARD's *hand,*
stopping him writing.

JANETTA: (*Voice over*) It wasn't coincidence. Something had
   changed. The phoney war was over . . .

(JANETTA *leans over and sits on the desk, putting her arms round*
him. She is dressed in pyjamas. LEONARD, *in profile, looks up at*
her as she looks down at him.)

That night I took Leonard to bed.

22. INT. LIBRARY. DAY

At once EVERNDEN, *crossing the central floor of the library with a*
large pile of books, totters and falls to the ground. The books go
spilling around him. The library is quite busy at midday and at once
the members turn round to see. First to see behind the desk is LESLEY.

LESLEY: What's that? Oh my God.

(*As she moves across* ASHCROFT, *the senior librarian, a thunder-*
browed man in his mid-sixties, is crossing from the other
direction, and clearing a path to EVERNDEN's *prostrate body.*)

ASHCROFT: Clear the way. Everyone, please make some room.

(ASHCROFT *loosens* EVERNDEN's *collar round his neck, and lifts*
his wrist to check for a pulse. There is now a circle of people
round EVERNDEN. LESLEY *and* JANETTA *have pushed through*
from the desk and now are kneeling opposite ASHCROFT.)

It looks like a heart attack.

JANETTA: Blow into his chest.

(ASHCROFT *looks at her a second. Then turns to an assistant.*)

ASHCROFT: Quick, get an ambulance.

JANETTA: Come on, turn him over, get on with it.
> (*She has taken hold of* EVERNDEN *and put him on his back, her arm round him. She finds herself directly opposite* ASHCROFT *across the body.* ASHCROFT *pauses, eye to eye with* JANETTA, *obviously reluctant to kiss* EVERNDEN. *So, impulsively, she reaches down and blows with surprising force into* EVERNDEN's *lungs. A second blast. A third.*)
> How we doing?
> (ASHCROFT *looks down, holding* EVERNDEN's *wrist.* JANETTA *blows a fourth time. A fifth, with less conviction. Then sits back, exhausted.* EVERNDEN *is dead in* ASHCROFT's *arms.*)

ASHCROFT: We've lost him. He's gone.

23. EXT. BAYSWATER. DAY

The peeling stucco façade of a large house in the back streets of Bayswater, broken up into flats. It looks in appalling conditon, almost derelict. At once the main door is opened by MRS GILL, *a painfully thin, small woman in her seventies, who comes to the door wearing an apron. There is a gloomy hall behind her, and the signs of multiple occupancy beyond.* JANETTA *is standing on the doorstep in her coat, carrying a black briefcase.*

JANETTA: Mr Evernden's things. I said I'd bring them over.

MRS GILL: Oh yes, thank you. We had a call from the library.
> (MRS GILL *passes* JANETTA, *leading her out of the doorway and past the railings to the steps which lead down to the basement. She leaves the front door open.*)
> We'll put them downstairs. Come down, why don't you?
> (*She starts painfully shuffling down the front steps.*)
> I don't quite know what we're going to do.

24. INT. EVERNDEN'S FLAT. DAY

A basement flat. Light only from a window below pavement level. The lights have been turned on, and the effect is bare, but quite warm. A standard lamp, a Victorian sofa, some china objects, a Victorian bookcase, a small stove at which he has cooked. Everything is formidably tidy. There is a card table, of green baize, at which there is an unfinished game of cards. MRS GILL *is on the move, looking for something, while* JANETTA *is standing, holding her briefcase, wondering what to do with it.*

MRS GILL: Put it down there.

> (JANETTA *puts the briefcase on Evernden's desk.*)

JANETTA: I wonder, do you know who's next of kin?

> (MRS GILL *has opened a wardrobe door and is peering in.*
> *Evernden's single bed is neat beside the wardrobe.*)

MRS GILL: I'm not sure.

JANETTA: He lived by himself?

MRS GILL: He did have a sister in Nottingham. I think she died about three years ago.

> (JANETTA *has moved to the green baize table, and idly picked up*
> *a card which is turned down, to see what's in the hand. It's an*
> *ace.*)

He liked to play cards. He had some friends he played cards with. I don't think there's anyone else.

> (MRS GILL *has opened a small cupboard beside the fireplace.*
> *There, inside, a black cat is sitting, its eyes wide.*)

He had Suzie. She's a stray really. But she liked Mr Evernden.

> (JANETTA *kneels down and looks in the cupboard.*)

JANETTA: I'll take Suzie home if you like.

25. EXT. BASEMENT STEPS. DAY

JANETTA *is coming up the steps, carrying Suzie.* MRS GILL *is behind*
her. As they come up, JULIUSZ *is approaching in his big brown coat.*
Behind him are a couple of other Poles. JULIUSZ *recognizes* JANETTA
as she comes up the steps.

JULIUSZ: Hello. How you doing? Just fancy seeing you here.

> (JANETTA *is stuck trying to get past* JULIUSZ *on the stairs.*
> *Mysteriously his friends are carrying large pieces of timber which*
> *they seem to be taking downstairs.*)

What a nice little pussy, eh? How are you, Mrs Gill?

> (JANETTA *has reached the pavement now. The door to*
> *Evernden's flat has been left open by* MRS GILL *to let the*
> *Poles in.*)

MRS GILL: Fine, thank you.

JULIUSZ: Keeping well?

MRS GILL: Yes, thank you.

> (JANETTA *frowns, left on the pavement.* MRS GILL *has passed*

JULIUSZ *and is heading back to the main door of the house.*
JULIUSZ *signals to his two friends who are waiting with the
timber.*)
JULIUSZ: So this is good, this is lovely, come on, lads, in you go.
(*They go into Evernden's.* JANETTA *turns and catches* MRS GILL
upstairs before she goes in.)
JANETTA: Who are they? Who's that?
MRS GILL: Oh, it's Mr Janowski.
JANETTA: What's he doing?
MRS GILL: Oh, he's looking after the place.
JANETTA: Looking after it?
(*Now* JULIUSZ *sticks his head out of the basement door again
and calls up to* MRS GILL.)
JULIUSZ: Mrs Gill!
MRS GILL: Yes.
(*She turns to go back down and join* JULIUSZ. JANETTA *is left
all by herself, bewildered and disturbed.*)
Thank you for coming. I've got to go.

26. INT. LEONARD'S ROOM. NIGHT

Suzie stretched on the bed beside JANETTA, *who is sitting back against
the wall, a coat round her shoulders.* LEONARD *reaches down and
hands her a mug of cocoa.*
LEONARD: There. You all right?
(*She nods slightly. He sits on the other end of the bed. She sips
her cocoa, thoughtful.*)
JANETTA: It was my first. He was there, then he wasn't.
LEONARD: Yes.
JANETTA: And the difference is only a breath.
(*She turns and looks at him.*)
It was just very shocking.
(*She turns back and strokes the cat, who looks entirely content in
her new surroundings.*)
I went to his flat. There was nothing there. It was awful. At
the end, he had nothing except a few objects. And a
collection of books.
LEONARD: Well? So what?
(JANETTA *frowns, not understanding.*)
You can't judge people's lives by the surface. (*He smiles.*) I

23

mean, look at us, what do we have? (*He pauses.*) Well, as it happens, we do have a salami.

JANETTA: Really?

LEONARD: Yes.

(*He rises and goes over to the desk.*)

I sold a poem.

(*He picks up the salami from the desk.*)

About my ship going down.

(*He puts the salami down and faces* JANETTA.)

But if a stranger walked in and looked round our lives, they'd say, 'Do you realize what they had? Between them? A single salami. How tragic!'

(*Moving towards her*) And yet we're not tragic at all.

JANETTA: No.

(*She looks at him a moment. He sits down on the chair arm again.*)

He died so suddenly. I don't know. He'd been saying recently how well he felt. How he wanted me to help him reorganize the library.

LEONARD: Have you heard how to make God laugh?

JANETTA: No.

LEONARD: Tell him your plans.

(*She thinks a moment, then smiles.*)

JANETTA: Yes. Yes, absolutely.

(LEONARD *is very quiet.* JANETTA *looks at him, as if knowing what's coming.*)

LEONARD: Tell me. What plans do you have?

(*They both smile. Then* JANETTA *reaches out and embraces him.*)

27. EXT. ROAD. DAY

Summer 1947. The repeated shot of the country lane, in blazing sun, as it was at the beginning of the film. Trees, open road.

JANETTA: (*Voice over*) We went to the beach, it was the first time I went there . . .

(LEONARD, *looking bookish and serious, walks beside* JANETTA, *full of laughter. For the first time we see them as a couple. The beach is revealed as they walk through the dunes.*)

24

28. EXT. BEACH. DAY

They are walking together side by side, the beach completely deserted around them, the dunes behind them.

JANETTA: (*Voice over*) We saved all our money to stay in a hotel. Summer came as we were driving. The winter ended in front of our eyes. And, for the first time, he talked about the war. (*He is thoughtful, quiet.*)

LEONARD: When you're going down, it's as if in slow motion. You can see the torpedo, as it's approaching. It's almost comic, in a way. You see it in the water and everything's suspended. You think, oh I see, here it comes. (*He looks at her a moment.*) It changes you. Before the war . . . (*He smiles.*) I was brought up, I was trained to be brilliant. Like the rest of my family. I played cricket, I would have a proper career. Running the country. It was simple, I was English. I thought the real world was real. (*JANETTA frowns.*)

JANETTA: What do you mean? You haven't lost your ambition?

LEONARD: No. But it's different.

JANETTA: It sounds like you're saying all your will has gone. (*He thinks a moment.*)

LEONARD: There's a smell. It's in the darkness. It's burning paintwork. And burning flesh. Then ether. (*He is thoughtful, not looking at her.*)

JANETTA: You don't talk about it much.

LEONARD: No. That's what poetry's for. To say what can't be said. (*JANETTA moves round and looks up at him, kisses him, more in love than we have ever seen her. They hold each other close.*)

29. INT. HOTEL. DAY

A plain hotel room. A double bed. JANETTA *and* LEONARD *are naked under the sheets, making love. Sunshine is beating through the thin curtains. They are totally rapt in each other, a long way into their lovemaking, when you hear the distant, insistent noise of a fire alarm.*
  LEONARD *frowns, but* JANETTA *makes a small noise of protest and*

takes hold of him to prevent him thinking about anything else.
    The noise stops for a second, then goes on.
LEONARD: What's that?
    (*She's firm.*)
JANETTA: It's nothing.
    (*There's a moment's pause.*)
    It's nothing. Come here.
    (*He moves down further into her. Her head goes back. His face,
    in absolute concentration.*)
    It's just practice.
    (*They smile slightly.*)
    They're just practising.
    (*Then* LEONARD *moves again. Whatever adjustment he makes is
    profoundly satisfying to them both.* JANETTA's *face in absolute
    abandon, his in joy.*)
    (*Then quietly*) Yes.

30. INT. HOTEL. DAY

*The bell is still ringing. A sudden battering at the door, violent, a hand
beating hard.*
    At once JANETTA *and* LEONARD *sit up in the bed, as the door is
flung open by the secret police. In fact it's a* CHAMBERMAID, *spry,
wiry, in her mid-fifties.*
    She starts screaming at them at the top of her voice.
CHAMBERMAID: What are you, monkeys? You people are
    disgusting. This place could burn down.
    (JANETTA *and* LEONARD *look in horror across the room, trying
    to cover their nakedness with the wet and crumpled sheet. The*
    CHAMBERMAID *moves towards them, and throws their clothes at
    them.*)
    You'd still be behaving like animals. Get up!
    Get out of here! Go on, get out!
    (*She goes. They burst out laughing, their clothes strewn across
    them.*)
JANETTA: (*Voice over*) I do remember I'd never felt closer to
    anyone. I felt I was wholly alive. I was free. That's what I
    felt. It's the only explanation. Everything happened at once.

31. INT. LIBRARY. DAY

At once, as if in answer to her voice over, IAN TYSON *speaks, leaning across the counter in the foyer of the library.*

IAN: It's the English, you know. They're frightened of energy.

    (JANETTA *looks up. She is sorting out books behind the counter.* IAN TYSON *is leaning across, apparently having spoken for no reason. He is looking even shinier than before, his face bonier, his skin whiter, his skull more transparent, his hair shinier. He is holding his hat in his hands.*)

JANETTA: What?

    (*She looks at him in bewilderment.*)

IAN: They hate it if you raise your voice. Why is everyone so quiet in libraries?

    (*He is looking hard at her. She is refusing to be charmed. When she speaks it is quietly, politely.*)

JANETTA: Politeness. Consideration for others.

    (IAN *leans across the counter a little more.*)

IAN: I want you to put those books down and just walk straight out the door.

JANETTA: What d'you mean?

IAN: With me.

    (*Before she can respond, he puts up a hand.*)

    Now don't make a scene.

JANETTA: I'm not making a scene.

IAN: Good.

    (*She is genuinely angry at this, but frightened to draw attention to herself by raising her voice. He is smiling.*)

    I know what you're thinking. You're thinking I'm not even attractive.

JANETTA: I wasn't.

IAN: Oh yes, you were.

    (*She is now finding it hard to look away from him.*)

    And now you're thinking . . . hang on, there's something about him. Actually, if you just stop and look . . . he's not as ugly as I thought he was . . .

    (*He trails off, smiling.* JANETTA *doesn't know how to react.*)

    I'm told women don't care about the physical, all they're looking for is a beautiful mind.

    (*He smiles, enjoying himself now.* JANETTA *has a reluctant smile*

27

coming on.)
Well, my mind is beautiful. I was five years in the army.
(*He reaches into his mackintosh pocket.*)
Here, I bought you a watch.
(*But from his pocket, he has untidily taken out a whole handful of silver watches, all with metal straps, a great bunch of them. He laughs.*)
Whoops, that was tacky . . . ?
JANETTA: (*Smiling*) *Five* watches?
IAN: I'm sorry. A girl likes to feel she's special, is that right? Is that your point?
(*She looks at him nervously. She looks round to see if anyone is overhearing this.*)
I'll do it again. Pretend I've just got the one.
(*And he repeats the action, only this time he takes just one watch out and speaks with sudden intimacy.*)
Here, I bought you a watch.
(JANETTA, *struck by his tone, turns and, relieved, sees* LESLEY *carrying a big pile of books under her chin.*)
JANETTA: Do you know my friend? This is Miss Perowne. This is Mr Tyson.
(LESLEY *frowns in bewilderment at this strange introduction. But* JANETTA *is now looking* IAN *full in the face.*)
Lesley will see to your needs.
(*And she turns and goes.*)

32. INT. READING ROOM, LIBRARY. DAY

JANETTA *is sitting alone on a staircase in the empty reading room. Her elbows on her knees, her hands on her chin. She is plainly just waiting, indecisive, scared, thoughtful.*

33. INT. LEONARD'S ROOM. NIGHT

LEONARD *is sitting in the armchair, reading.* JANETTA *is trying to read a book on the bed. But she shifts. And* LEONARD *looks up.*
LEONARD: What's going on? You seem restless.
JANETTA: Do I?
LEONARD: Is something wrong?
(*He frowns, waiting for her to answer.*)
Please say if there is.

JANETTA: No.
>   (*There's a silence, him waiting for her.*)
>   It's just . . . I don't know . . . can we go back to the coast?
LEONARD: Go back? We only just left.
JANETTA: I know. It's just . . . the beach was so wonderful.
LEONARD: Yes.
>   (*He is looking at her, very level, clear-eyed.*)
>   Well, it was.
JANETTA: I don't know. I'm not at ease in London.
LEONARD: No. (*He waits a moment.*) No, I see that. (*He smiles
>   slightly.*) Is there a reason?
JANETTA: No reason.
>   (*He looks down, avoiding her now.*)
LEONARD: What about our jobs?
JANETTA: Oh, I can get off. For a few days. Can't you?
>   (*He shrugs slightly, refusing to reply. But it is hard for her to tell
>   from his unreadable manner how curious he is about this sudden
>   nervousness in her.*)
>   It's an instinct. I simply feel . . . we should go now.
LEONARD: Now?
>   (*She backs off a little, alarmed that she is too insistent.*)
JANETTA: Or tomorrow. Anyway, quickly.
>   (*He looks at the writing in front of him, not giving anything
>   away.*)
LEONARD: (*Quietly*) Of course. Whatever you say.

34. INT. LEONARD'S ROOM. DAY

JANETTA *is lying asleep in bed. There is daylight at the window.*
LEONARD *is at his desk and takes a plain white card on which he
writes with his fountain pen. He shakes the card dry, then walks across
the room and puts the card on the pillow next to* JANETTA, *where we
read it.*

>   CAN'T GO AWAY. WOULD LOVE TO. WE WILL LATER.
>   SEE YOU TONIGHT. L.

LEONARD *picks up his briefcase and goes out, closing the door.*

35. EXT. STREET, BLOOMSBURY. DAY

JANETTA *walking down the street, seen in close-up, from two different angles. First, we are to one side of her. She is moving quickly, not quite as if being pursued, but almost. There is a London square behind her, trees. Then we are in front of her. We see the slight tension on her face. A car driving along beside her. You can tell, you know that a voice will call out to her. And it does.*

IAN: (*Out of shot*) Hey, there you are. I've been looking for you.
(JANETTA *stops. Then she turns.* IAN *is sitting in a black Austin, leaning out of the window beside her. He's by himself.*)

JANETTA: Yes.

IAN: Where have you been? You haven't been at the library.
(*She looks at him a moment, mistrustfully.*)

JANETTA: I said I was ill.
(*He is all cheery good humour.*)

IAN: So what have you been doing?

JANETTA: Do you really want to know?

IAN: Yes.
(*She is standing just staring at him now. He shrugs.*)
Yes, for God's sake. Of course. Get in and tell me.

JANETTA: I'm telling you here.
(*She waits a moment. Then concedes.*)
I've been tracking round London.

IAN: What, to avoid me?
(*She looks down, not answering.* IAN *is smiling.*)
Get in.

JANETTA: No.

IAN: Please get in. I'd like you to.
(JANETTA *hesitates.*)
It's nothing dangerous. I'm just a man.

36. EXT. STREET. DAY

A huge bomb site backing on to the backs of big houses. Gangs of children playing with a huge hoop which they are driving across the bomb site, shouting and screaming.

IAN: Everyone is going to want property. They just don't know it yet. It's the Englishman's dream. Buy a house, close the door, stop history.
(IAN's *point of view as he looks up at the huge decaying properties going by.* IAN *is driving in the Austin, talking cheerfully, his hands on the wheel.*)

No more incidents. It's all they want, now they're back from the war. Build a little box and shut yourself in it. (*He smiles.*) Everyone's had enough of events.

37. EXT. STREET. DAY

IAN *gets out of the car on to the pavement and walks down the street,* JANETTA *following, among old women carrying their shopping, the transients on the steps, the poor children playing among themselves. The scene darkening slightly now in the late afternoon.*

IAN: The future belongs to anyone who's realized. Get in there early, that's my advice. Buy a house.

JANETTA: I can't afford it.

IAN: You don't need any money. Borrow.

JANETTA: I've nothing to borrow against. (*She frowns.*) Don't you need security?

IAN: Security? (*He says the word as if he's never heard it before in his life.*) I have no idea what you mean.

38. INT. CLUB. DAY

Down the tiny dark stairway, and into the Empire Club. It is the barest basement room, with no natural light, just some red shades over light bulbs and a bare wooden floor. Round and about they have placed bare wooden tables and chairs, and there is in one corner a piano and in the other a small bar, with an old man with thick black hair and a black cotton jacket. There are about thirty people drinking, mostly Polish, mostly men; but there are also a few blacks in one corner, and a couple of women by themselves. The place is thick with smoke and conversation. JULIUSZ *is, as usual, in his thick coat, he gets up to greet* IAN, *but* IAN *doesn't pause for a second, crossing the room.*

JULIUSZ: Ian. There you are, we've been waiting for you. We need some decisions.

(IAN *is heading for an intense young man who is sitting by himself in the corner, and doesn't even pause to look round.*)

IAN: You know Janetta, of course?

(JULIUSZ *opens both arms in greeting.*)

JULIUSZ: Janetta!

(*It's impossible to tell whether he does or not, and* IAN *has*

31

already sat down at the table opposite the young man, ROMAN, *who is very thin, with a long nose and thick Polish accent.*)

ROMAN: I got you a terrace. Six houses in Powys Gardens.

(JULIUSZ *has moved next to* IAN *and has put his foot on* IAN's *chair, leaning over him now, so that* IAN *barely has to look up.* JANETTA *watches, a few feet away.*)

JULIUSZ: Powys Gardens is good.

ROMAN: I got another in Talbot Road.

(IAN *smiles, and is reaching into his pocket.*)

IAN: Not Talbot Road. Lexington Gardens is my limit. Nothing east of that.

(*He has taken out a great roll of money, all in notes, which he is beginning to count. He is smiling.*)

That way no one gets hurt.

(ROMAN *puts down the deeds of the properties on the table.* JANETTA *only just catches sight of this, as* JULIUSZ *has put his arm round her to shepherd her to the bar, as if he doesn't want her there for the actual exchange of money.*)

JULIUSZ: Come and get a beer.

JANETTA: Won't he go and see them? Is he buying houses? Doesn't he see them?

(JULIUSZ *is leaning against the bar now, smiling at the barman. He turns to* JANETTA.)

JULIUSZ: Beer?

JANETTA: What? Oh yes, beer's fine.

(*She looks across to the table.* IAN *is handing* ROMAN *the money and scooping up the deeds into his pocket.* JULIUSZ *has dealt with the barman, and now looks too.*)

JULIUSZ: He doesn't need to see them. Roman won't cheat him. Roman wants to do business with him again.

(JANETTA *turns to look at* JULIUSZ *to try and judge the weight of this remark, but as she does* IAN *slips alongside her. She turns, surprised.*)

JANETTA: Don't you have an office?

IAN: Why? This is my office. Everyone knows.

(*He smiles, spreading his arms wide. No drink, just hanging out, as in a familiar element, looking round the room.*)

From five till six, they can get me here.

(*He nods at a telephone with coinbox in the corner, attached to the wall on a piece of black wood. As soon as* JANETTA *looks at*

it, it starts ringing. Nobody moves to answer it. IAN *smiles.*)
There, you see. I'm opening up shop.

39. INT. CLUB. EVENING

*Later. A heavily peroxided blonde is singing love songs in Polish,
accompanied by an older man at the piano. The place is fuller. Then
we see* IAN *at work on the phone in the corner. He is chattering
animatedly, nodding, totally absorbed in his work.* JANETTA *has
relaxed by the bar, enjoying it, moving in rhythm to the music, looking
round, taking it all in.* JULIUSZ *is beside her, looking after her. Now
he smiles.*

JULIUSZ: You know what Ian says?
JANETTA: No.
    (*She smiles back, a tiny bit boozy with it all.*)
    No, tell me.
JULIUSZ: He says when a business builds a headquarters then you
    know it's the beginning of the end. (*He smiles.*) It's . . . what
    the word he says . . . *decadent.*
JANETTA: (*Nods.*) Uh-huh.
JULIUSZ: Because then it's about all the wrong things. Executive
    karsies. What colour you have to be painting the walls.
JANETTA: Yes.
    (*They both smile. She is flushed. It is suddenly very relaxed.*)
JULIUSZ: Ian has a theory.
JANETTA: On yes? What's the theory?
JULIUSZ: 'Dobry interes powinien zawsze być giętki.' (*He grins
    and translates.*) 'Good business should be light on its feet.'
    (*And at once* IAN *appears beside them, very cheerful.*)
IAN: And now that's over.
    (JANETTA *nods at the phone, which has started ringing again. It
    does not occur to anyone else to answer it.*)
    Leave it. They should know. It's past six o'clock. (*He
    watches the phone ring a moment, serious now.*) That's the thing
    about me. I know when to stop.

40. INT. CLUB. NIGHT

Later. It is busier, but IAN *and* JANETTA *have cleared a corner to
themselves. The smoke is thicker, the singer has gone and there is just a*

pianist. Some empty bottles in front of them.

IAN: You see there's thousands of people flooding into London, where do they go? No one gives a toss. (*He smiles.*) You think bloody Belgravia'll take them? Even if they could afford it?

JANETTA: What, so you buy places and then do them up?
(IAN *frowns.*)

IAN: Do them up? No. Are you crazy?

JANETTA: Why?

IAN: Because if you spend money tarting places over, then you have to charge more rent, just to get your money back. Then people can't afford them. (*He smiles at the neatness of the logic.*) All you've got is another Belgravia. And that's no use to anyone. No, keeps thing basic.

JANETTA: How basic?

IAN: Pleasant. Basic. (*He looks round. Then thinks again.*) Basic. Cheap.

41. EXT. ALLEYWAY. NIGHT

JANETTA *and* IAN *come strolling out together into a wide alleyway by the club. It is like the side of a cinema, high-walled and dark, with metal fire escapes on one side, and the back doors of shops and restaurants on the other.*

JANETTA *is walking beside* IAN, *as they head away from the club.*

JANETTA: Hold on just a moment, where are we going?
(*She stops. He stands, mystified.*)

IAN: What does it matter? (*He shrugs slightly.*) We're going back to my place.

JANETTA: No. No, I have to go home. There's a man I live with.
(IAN *just frowns, as if this sounds too silly for words.*)
Don't you want to know more?

IAN: Do I? Not really.
(*She waits for him to say more. But he has nothing to add. She becomes more serious.*)

JANETTA: You know there's no question of my sleeping with you.
(*Again, he doesn't respond.*)
You do understand that? I haven't misled you.
(*There's another silence. It unnerves* JANETTA.)
It's out of the question, you've always known that.
(IAN *looks at her and smiles slightly.*)

34

IAN: Well, I can see that you think that you're a nice person. And if you slept with me, it might not seem to be kind. So you'd have to find a way of thinking it was right, really. I mean you'd have to tell yourself a good story. (*He smiles again.*) Or else it would spoil your idea of yourself.

(JANETTA *frowns, not understanding.*)

JANETTA: That's nothing to do with it. I don't want to hurt Leonard.

(*Again,* IAN *says nothing, but* JANETTA *answers as if he'd spoken.*)

He's a poet. I live in his room.

IAN: Uh-huh.

JANETTA: Or rather, he wants to be. He wants to express what he saw in the war. It's hard. There was so much suffering. Half of him is sorrowful. The other half is, you know, really quite hardened.

(*She frowns, thinking about it. He says nothing, not showing any reaction to her* naïveté.)

He's trying to work out what he believes.

(IAN *just nods slightly.*)

IAN: And you think that matters?

JANETTA: Of course. More than anything.

(*She looks at him a moment.*)

What we believe? Yes of course. *Of course.*

(*She stops, her disbelief growing. The two of them standing apart in the alley,* IAN *by a metal staircase, she in the middle of the alley.*)

It's terribly important.

IAN: Is it?

(*He looks at her a moment, as if really taking her in for the first time. Then he moves decisively away from the metal staircase.*)

I must go home.

(*She suddenly begins to panic at the idea of the conversation being left where it is.*)

JANETTA: Now look . . .

IAN: Do you need a lift somewhere?

JANETTA: You can't go now.

(*She runs after him down the alley. He turns round, surprised, amused. She catches him up and grabs him.*)

What did you mean? A moment ago? About it not mattering what we believe?

(*He looks at her a moment, as if deciding whether to explain to her. Then, his tone changes; he moves a couple of steps back towards her.*)

IAN: It's up to you. You can waste your life sitting there with your poet. I've met these kind of people. 'Oh, I think this; oh, I think that . . .' (*He spreads his arms, dramatizing.*) 'Oh, I feel; oh, I don't feel . . .' Of course it's fine. It's a great game. Especially for two players. (*He is suddenly serious.*) But don't ever kid yourself it's anything else.
(IAN *suddenly seems almost angry.*)
You're lucky, you're privileged. Spend your life asking, 'What do I *feel* about this? Do I *feel* I'm doing the right thing . . .' (*He pauses.*) Or else you can just do it. I know which kind of person I like.
(*There are tears in* JANETTA'*s eyes now.*)

JANETTA: That isn't fair.

IAN: You're free. Tell yourself stories. Why not? Most people do. I know why you came with me this evening. I also know what you'd be getting from me.
(*He is now standing right in front of her; she is trapped against the wall. She looks at him, fearful.*)

JANETTA: What's that?
(*He's smiling again.*)

IAN: No nonsense.
(IAN *smiles as if nothing could be simpler.*)
That's not nothing. Actually that's quite a lot.
(JANETTA *looks down.*)

JANETTA: Yes, I can see that. (*She smiles.*) And what do you think you'd be getting from me?
(*He looks at her for a moment, enjoying the silent answer he is giving, as if the whole thing were too obvious to be said out loud. Then he takes out a card and writes a telephone number on it. He hands it to her.*)

IAN: You know where I am. Five to six. You can find me like everyone else.

42. INT. LEONARD'S ROOM. NIGHT

At once JANETTA'*s face on the pillow, lying beside a sleeping* LEONARD. *She is staring straight ahead of her, then her eyes go*

36

towards LEONARD. *She lifts herself up and begins quietly to kiss the
back of his neck. He stirs, turning his face and burying his face in her.*
   *We see her face now on his shoulder. There are tears in her eyes as
she holds him. And then she speaks.*

JANETTA: (*Voice over*) What excuse shall I give? Isn't there always
   a reason?

43. INT. LIBRARY. DAY

JANETTA *is at her desk apparently absorbed in her work.*
   The place is quite busy. JANETTA *is checking through the card index
for a customer.*

JANETTA: (*Voice over*) Or at least can't we always think of one?
   Say, for instance, let's say: I wanted to understand him.
   (*She looks up casually to the clock on the wall of the library. It
   says five past five.*)
   I had to get close to find out what made him tick.
   (*She slips out from behind the desk and heads across the foyer of
   the library. By the wall, we see her destination: a wall telephone.
   She lifts it and begins to dial.*)
   Or else say: I lacked experience. I wanted to be out in the
   world, see people, get close to real life.

44. EXT. STREET. EVENING/INT. IAN'S BUILDING.EVENING

JANETTA *walking along the darkening streets by the back of Ladbroke
Grove. Dereliction, abandoned buildings, bomb sites, the poor
children playing in the streets.*

JANETTA: (*Voice over*) Say that, say either. Give a reason.
   Whichever you like.
   (*She comes to a big garage door and pushes it open. There is a
   vacated factory floor inside, deserted, with a small wooden
   staircase going up one side with a metal grille on one side.*)
   I can tell myself why I did what I did. But do I believe it?
   Did I ever?
   (*She starts to walk up the wooden staircase, looking upward to a
   bare, closed door at the top.*)
   Who knows? It served, for a time.

45. INT. IAN'S PLACE. NIGHT

JANETTA *lying abandoned in a double bed, by herself. She is lit only by the ambient light from the night outside. There is nothing in the warehouse-like space except the bed itself. It is obvious from the twist of the blanket that two people have just made love. But* JANETTA *is alone.*

After a moment, she gets up and wraps the blanket around her to go over to the plywood partition that separates the room the bed is in from the rest of the space. We are in industrial premises off Ladbroke Grove. IAN *has set his things down in them, so there is just a massive floor and a row of uncurtained windows, thick with grime. It is an early version of loft living: but with no concessions.* IAN *has tried to make it as much like an army barracks as possible. At the far end of the room, there are filing cabinets, with a prominent pin-up of Rita Hayworth on the side of them. A couple of tables, a few hard chairs. Acres of space.*

Wrapped in the blanket, JANETTA *looks across the space to where* IAN *is sitting, cross-legged on the floor. He is naked except for the old jacket over his shoulders. He is playing patience.*

JANETTA: You got up so quickly.

IAN: Yes.

> (*He goes on playing cards.*)

JANETTA: You wouldn't stay beside me.

> (*He looks at her a moment, then goes back to playing cards.* JANETTA *does not move from the doorway. There is ten yards between them.*)
>
> Why was that?

IAN: Because you didn't give yourself.

> (*There is a silence.* JANETTA *wraps the blanket tighter round her.*)

JANETTA: I don't know what you mean.

IAN: You know perfectly well.

> (*He goes on playing cards.*)

JANETTA: What? Give myself? What on earth does that mean?

> (*He smiles and looks at her now.*)

IAN: You don't know what give yourself means? Like – *give yourself?*

> (*He looks at her, then resumes his game.*)
>
> You do what you like. If that's all you want. When you make

love. Just to give a little. Just to lend yourself. But if that's what you want, I'm not your man.

(*She is looking down on him on the floor. The immense distances of the factory around them. The night outside the window, the cards going down silently.* JANETTA *holding the blanket to her.*)

JANETTA: What do *you* want?

IAN: I want you to give yourself. It's better.

(*There's a silence.*)

JANETTA: Come here.

(*She stays looking at him. There is a long silence. We are on her face, as we hear the sound, finally, of him getting up from the floor and moving towards her. Her expression barely changing as . . .*)

JANETTA: (*Voice over*) And so things changed, I stayed late with Ian . . .

46. INT. HOUSE. DAY

Montage. JANETTA *standing alone on the landing of a multi-occupancy house in North Kensington. We are above her, looking down, as she knocks on a filthy door. An* OLD WOMAN *opens it.*

JANETTA: Excuse me . . .

(*Now we are inside the dirty and derelict room as the* OLD WOMAN *heads towards us to go to the mantelpiece.*)

JANETTA: (*Voice over*) Then next day, Juliusz called me at the library; did I have a spare couple of hours? Which I did.

(*The* OLD WOMAN *calls to her unseen husband in another room.*)

OLD WOMAN: Hey Albert, they've sent a girl for the rent.

(JANETTA, *hovering at the door, smiles.*)

She sounds like she's at the university . . .

(*Now we are in another room, this time a family flat with six filthy children running about, sitting on the table, their harassed mother trying to control them.* JANETTA *looking on in the middle of the room.*)

JANETTA: (*Voice over*) And people seemed pleased to see me, I was surprised, I began to think, well this is actually fun . . .

(*Now she is back on the landing, checking her list with an easy professionalism. Knocking at the next door.*)

I get out and see things, it's interesting . . .

(*When she gets no answer, she frowns. Searches above the door frame.*)

I'll only do it once. How did Ian guess I'd actually enjoy it? . . .

(*Then she has an inspiration. She stoops down and lifts the linoleum to take out a ten-shilling note from underneath.*)

Perhaps he understands me.

47. INT. LEONARD'S ROOM. EVENING

JANETTA *is happily unpacking the contents of a carrier bag in the larder area.* LEONARD *is stooped over the gas ring in the main room, cooking something in the pan.* JANETTA *is very cheerful.*

LEONARD: You seem very well.

JANETTA: Yes, I'm fine.

(*She comes through to lay the table with two toothmugs, plates, a couple of knives and forks, and the bottle she has just unpacked, which she shows to* LEONARD.)

I bought us a treat. I went to buy gin.

LEONARD: Well, I went to buy parsnips.

(*He stands a moment, pan in hand now.*)

Gin and parsnips?

JANETTA: Perfect.

(*They both laugh. He comes over to put the pan on the table. She smiles at him. He sits down.*)

So tell me. How was your day?

48. INT. IAN'S PLACE. DAY

JANETTA *enters, puts her suitcase down and walks in. We see Ian's place for the first time by day.*

IAN *is sitting at a table, right by the filing cabinet, his back to us – just as* LEONARD'*s back has been to us previously, but this time across the vast spaces of the factory floor. He has piles of rent books on the table and a small notebook on which he is making little marks.*

He turns, hearing her near him.

IAN: What's this?

(*She stands a moment.*)

JANETTA: I thought I'd drop by.

IAN: You didn't tell me.

JANETTA: Why, no.

(*She smiles, a little mystified by his response as she approaches him. He is just sitting in his chair, dressed in vest and trousers, staring at her impassively.*)

What's wrong?

IAN: What did you come for?

JANETTA: For?

IAN: Yes.

JANETTA: I came to see you.

IAN: What, you like rent-collecting that much?

(*She has stopped, sensing the strangeness of his reaction to her sudden arrival. He is still looking at her, deadpan.*)

JANETTA: Yes. I mean, yes, that as well.

IAN: As well as what?

(*He looks at her directly, challenging.*)

No, I'm interested. Why don't you say?

(*She frowns, backtracking now, trying to make light of it.*)

JANETTA: Look, perhaps I shouldn't have done this. Aren't you pleased to see me? I made an excuse. I got off for three days.

IAN: Three days? You're here for three days?

JANETTA: Yes.

IAN: Good.

(IAN *gets up from his desk, impassive still, and hands her a whole stack of rent books.*)

You can take these. Go on. Get out there. Don't you want to do it?

(*She looks down, lost.*)

JANETTA: Well, I don't know.

(*He moves away across the room to get a shirt which is hanging from a filing cabinet at the far side.*)

What's wrong? Don't you want me? Don't you want to see me?

(*He doesn't turn to look at her as he puts on his shirt.*)

IAN: Have you left your boyfriend?

JANETTA: Why no.

(*He turns, suddenly right on the nail.*)

Not exactly.

IAN: Why not?

JANETTA: Why not?

IAN: Yes.

JANETTA: Do you want me to?

IAN: No.

> (*She looks down again.*)

JANETTA: I love him.

> (IAN *smiles, pleased with this, and moves towards her, on his way to crossing the room again.*)

IAN: Good, well, that's better. Now we're getting somewhere. You love him but you want to sleep with me.

> (*She is suddenly angry now.*)

JANETTA: I think I'd better go.

IAN: Good.

JANETTA: What is this? What on earth is this?

> (*She is standing, furious now. But* IAN *is angrily facing her.*)

IAN: Oh sure, yes, go back to your boyfriend. Why not? (*He shakes his head.*) Go and stand beside him. Isn't that what you're there for? Look good as you walk into a pub. Where he goes to discuss the meaning of things. With you on his arm. So he gets some glory. A nice young girl. Who he hopes everyone notices.

> (*He looks at her from across the room with contempt.*)

Because he wants to be seen with you. What, does he say you're the reason he writes his poems?

> (JANETTA'*s expression shows at once that* IAN *is right, but before she can speak* IAN *has jumped in.*)

You see! You help *him* with his work.

JANETTA: So what? (*She suddenly raises her voice.*) So what?

IAN: Don't you have any pride? Who are you? Do you always want to be someone who just tags along?

> (*He turns at the far end of the room, his manner changing.*)

Now the difference is, I believe women can actually do it. I asked you yesterday to go and do a job.

JANETTA: I did. I did it.

IAN: Why do you think I did that? Why do you think I sent you out by yourself? (*He stops a moment, his tone softening.*) Because I believe in you. You could make a contribution. I mean it. You could be someone in your own right. I'd give you an area. You'd run it. You have a gift, you know that?

> (*He has moved towards her, quieter now.*)

You could actually do well at this work.

> (*She looks at him, not knowing what he will say next, a little mistrustful as he comes near.*)

42

But you'd have to want it. You know what that means. You'd
have to stop lying. (*He smiles slightly.*) I can't work with people
who tell themselves lies.
(*He is opposite her now, very quiet. She does not move.*)
'I love Leonard, but I want to sleep with Ian.' (*He smiles
again.*) Go on, say it.
JANETTA: Out loud?
IAN: No. You don't have to do that.
(*There is silence. Then very quietly he repeats the sentence.*)
'I love Leonard, but I want to sleep with Ian.'
(*We look at* JANETTA *as she says it to herself. When she has, she
smiles slightly.*)
JANETTA: I've said it.
IAN: Right. (*He smiles now.*) There's no problem.
(*He moves right into her, his mouth right by her ear.*)
So sleep with me.
(*He moves his cheek across her cheek. She tips her head back a
little. He is very quiet.*)
And then we'll go collecting some rents.

49. EXT. STREET. DAY

IAN, *this time driving a different car, draws up outside a big stucco-
fronted terrace. He is in an open-topped sports car, with* JANETTA
beside him and JULIUSZ *sitting good-naturedly on the top in the back.
No sooner does he draw up, than* IAN *jumps out, talking all the while.*
JANETTA: (*Voice over*) There were three days, I then had three days
with Ian, I never had a clue where we'd be going next . . .
(IAN *has got out, talking, and is heading for the front door of one of
the houses, oblivious of whether* JANETTA *can get out of a car
without opening the door.*)
IAN: Now I want you to see this, it's kind of historic. I took it from
this man. He had no idea. Do you know how much I paid?
JANETTA: No.
(*She is looking puzzled, as* JULIUSZ *has gone round to the boot of
the car, and is getting out metal pails which is is setting down on the
pavement as he closes the boot again.*)
IAN: Fifty pounds. Every penny of my demob money. It was the
very first house I bought.
(JULIUSZ *has picked up the pails and is walking beside* JANETTA

43

towards the house, as IAN *gets out a huge ring of keys to look for the right one.*)

JULIUSZ: All the time, you know, Ian and I, we were in the hills outside Florence.

(IAN *grins at the door.*)

IAN: We were stuck for eight months.

JULIUSZ: (*Grins.*) Yes, that's right.

JANETTA: You were in the army?

JULIUSZ: That's right.

JANETTA: Together?

JULIUSZ: Why, yes.

(*The group are all standing at the door, waiting for* IAN *and the keys. The two men have smiles on their faces, quite private, at the memory of the time.*)

You should have been there. It was bloody awful.

(*He sets down the pails on the porch.* JANETTA *looks down. They are full of coins. She frowns.* IAN *has opened the door and turns back for a second.*)

IAN: But I always said, when I get back, there's going to be a business. And I'm going to go for it.

(*He disappears inside with the pails.* JULIUSZ *smiles.*)

JULIUSZ: And my golly, that's what he did.

50. INT. BASEMENT. DAY

Darkness. At once IAN *pulls the string which turns on a bare light bulb. We are in a dark passageway and there are four doors off it. The walls and doors have been newly jerry-built in unpainted wood – little more than improvised partitions. The space is crammed in front of them with clothes, beds on the floor and the remains of meals.* IAN *and* JANETTA *look at it together.*

IAN: Poverty – ugh! – don't you hate it? Every morning I wake up and think, never again.

(JANETTA *stands still behind him, looking in.*)

I'm not frightened of it. I'll go back to it if I have to. (*He smiles.*) But I don't have to. So I'm all right.

(*He moves across the room and heads towards the meter in the far corner.* JANETTA *is looking round now, struck by the mantelpiece in front of her. It is of ornate stone, but has been cut in half by the new partition wall, making it meaningless. The fireplace has also*

44

been sliced in two. Beside it, she frowns at the little cupboard where she found Suzie. Now it is filled with spilling garbage. IAN *is opening the meter with one of a huge bunch of keys.*)

JANETTA: Hold on, I didn't realize. Before . . . I came in a different entrance.

(IAN *has opened the meter box, put down the keys. She looks round.*)

This was Mr Evernden's. I've been here before.

(JULIUSZ *arrives in the doorway.*)

JULIUSZ: It was too big. One old man sleeping by himself.

(JULIUSZ *goes.* JANETTA *looks at* IAN, *holding his gaze.*)

JANETTA: It seems a shame. It was nice here.

(IAN *looks back at her. Pause.*)

Where next?

51. INT. LONDON AUCTION HOUSE. DAY

At once we see IAN *and* JANETTA *bounding together through the entrance hall that leads to the London Auction Market;* IAN *in a state of high excitement.*

JANETTA: (*Voice over*) There was never a time when he wasn't testing me, it was like he was trying to see how far I'd go . . .

(*We follow them into the auction rooms, which are bare but for large wall mirrors at either end. The room is full of smoke with a hundred bidders, mostly Jewish, in dark coats and black hats. At one end an* AUCTIONEER *is scanning the room for bids, amid a tremendous hubbub of bidders trying to make themselves heard.* JANETTA *takes a seat while* IAN *walks up to the* AUCTIONEER'S CLERK. *Across the room is a younger man in a blue suit, the leader of the Stamford Hill Cowboys, who acknowledges* IAN's *arrival.*)

STAMFORD HILL COWBOY: Reb Tyson.

(IAN *looks at him, says nothing and returns to* JANETTA.)

52. INT. AUCTION HOUSE. DAY

Later. IAN *is now at the centre with his schedule for the auction;* JANETTA *is the only woman in this all-male crowd.* IAN *explodes in an orgy of indignation:*

IAN: Come on! You can't be serious!

(*He turns away in mock agony, now shouting at the* AUCTIONEER.)

Two hundred for a terraced house in Kentish Town!

AUCTIONEER: Two hundred pounds, Mr Tyson, is the reserve.

IAN: Are you going out of your head?

(IAN *suddenly turns to* JANETTA *and leads her quickly away from the bidding, his hand on her arm.*)

Dip out.

JANETTA: What?

IAN: Come on.

JANETTA: Are you not buying that one?

IAN: Of course not. You make a lot of fuss about the ones you don't want. It confuses the Stamford Hill Cowboys.

(*In the background the Stamford Hill Cowboys are still bidding loudly.*)

JANETTA: Goodness. Is that what they're called?

IAN: Look, the whole thing's a lottery. You're buying a title. It's just an address. You haven't seen it. You go there, you find you've bought a bombsite. You've paid forty quid for a façade. Or maybe not. Maybe it's a really nice house. Undamaged.

(*He looks beyond her back to the auction.*)

JANETTA: How do you know?

IAN: How do you *know*? (*He smiles.*) How do you think? That's the talent.

(*And he starts moving her quickly back towards the action.*)

Come on, the next one's a really good one.

(*He hands her the auction list.*)

Bid for me, will you?

JANETTA: Bid?

IAN: Yes. Bid. BID. I won't be long. Lots 408, 470, and 532. And make sure you get them . . .

(*He pushes away through the crowd, greeting friends, rapidly disappearing in the press.*)

53. INT. AUCTION HOUSE. DAY

A few moments later. JANETTA *is bidding excitedly.*

JANETTA: Three hundred! Three hundred!

(*The* STAMFORD HILL COWBOY *lifts his paper on the other side of the room.*)

STAMFORD HILL COWBOY: Three ten.

(JANETTA *responds at once.*)

JANETTA: Three twenty.

STAMFORD HILL COWBOY: Three thirty.

(*The* AUCTIONEER *looks straight back at* JANETTA, *who does not bid, but just returns his stare.*)

AUCTIONEER: Anything above three thirty? Three thirty? No? No?

(JANETTA *waits, perfectly cool, then at the last possible moment, just before it's sold . . .*)

JANETTA: Three forty.

(*And the* AUCTIONEER *shouts in triumph.*)

AUCTIONEER: Three *forty*, I hear.

54. INT. AUCTION HOUSE. DAY

A few moments later. JANETTA *is jumping up and down with excitement at* IAN's *return, pushing his way back through the crowd.*

JANETTA: I got it! I got it!

IAN: Of course you got it, I should bloody well hope so. How much?

(*He puts his arm round her to lead her away.*)

JANETTA: Three forty.

(IAN *smiles and moves right in to her cheek, as if for an intimacy.*)

IAN: It'll be a thousand by the end of the year.

(*Then he's away, taking her arm and pushing her off through the crowd of screaming people.*)

(JANETTA *and* IAN *are lost under the voice over: gesticulating figures, threading their way through the crowd.*)

JANETTA: (*Voice over*) It was a kind of craziness. It was infectious. He was always pushing. He pushed all the time.

55. EXT. AUCTION HOUSE. DAY

IAN *and* JANETTA *come out of the auction house. In the street a beggar is sitting on the pavement, leaning against the wall.* JANETTA *smiles at* IAN, *who is high as a kite from the proceedings inside.*

JANETTA: Give this man some money.

IAN: No.

JANETTA: What? Why?
   (*They have passed the man and are several yards on.* JANETTA *stops.*)
JANETTA: I'll give him some money.
IAN: Don't do it.
   (IAN *turns and looks at her, silent, angry.*)
JANETTA: Yes, I will. Yes. I bloody well will.
   (*She is fishing in her handbag for cash.* IAN *just looks at her.*)
IAN: You don't give him money because you care about him. You do it to make yourself feel good. You're buying self-esteem. For cash.
   (*She stops fishing and looks at him. He is quiet, contemptuous.*)
   It's disgusting.
JANETTA: Oh, really?
   (*She takes a few steps towards the beggar and reaches down to put money in his hand.* IAN *watches, not moving. The beggar thanks her.* JANETTA *walks back to* IAN, *who has not moved.*)
   He needs help. And now he's got it. What difference does it make *why*?
   (IAN *is already shaking his head.*)
IAN: Because a worse thing happens. You begin to tell yourself lies. About who you are.
   (JANETTA'*s eyes are narrowing; she is determined to stand up to him.*)
JANETTA: Why are you so threatened?
   (*He doesn't answer.*)
   Why are you so frightened when I do something kind?
   (*He looks at her. Then he walks across to the beggar. He reaches into his pocket. He unrolls a wad of notes and lets some flutter down. Then he looks at* JANETTA, *not moving from the man.*)
IAN: Am I a nice person now?

56. EXT. ALLEYWAY. NIGHT

Down the darkened alley comes a group of five men. At their centre, a large bald man, DEREK GREEN, *in his early sixties, cockney, with a younger black girl on his arm. Around him, keeping close, is a group of men in coats, one of whom is extremely tall and wide. They move as a group.*
   Then from the club entrance come IAN *and* JANETTA. IAN *sees the*

group moving towards the club entrance, and he stops.
  The group stops opposite him.
IAN: Well, my goodness, my friend, how are you?
  (DEREK *just smiles at him, not answering. Like an animal, the*
  girl holds his arm tighter, as if by instinct.)
DEREK: Still at it, Ian?
IAN: I am.
DEREK: Buying houses?
IAN: Yeah.
  (*Only* IAN *and* DEREK *are smiling. The big men around* DEREK
  look more serious. The alley is otherwise deserted.)
  And you, Derek? Still in London? I heard you were buying
  golf clubs in Walton Heath.
DEREK: (*Referring to three enormous thugs beside him.*) Dennis is
  trying to lower his handicap. So I decided to buy him a
  course.
  (IAN *smiles.*)
IAN: What I heard, you also had a race-track. And a couple of
  cinemas. All this leisure stuff, sounds like you're planning
  for retirement.
DEREK: I don't think so, Ian. I've got a long way to go. I'm going
  to die in my bed. Smelling of sticky young women and
  caviare.
  (IAN *pauses just a second.*)
IAN: And do you buy those as well?
  (*There's a second's pause.* DENNIS *is just intelligent enough to*
  know DEREK *has been insulted. Derek's tone changes.*)
DEREK: You want to be careful. You know that, Ian? We all
  heard you had a good war. (*Smiles slightly.*) But the army's
  protection. This is peacetime. Now you're exposed.
  (IAN *doesn't answer. Just looks at him.*)
  I own a few music halls, if you want to work as a comedian.
IAN: Well, thank you Derek.
  (DEREK *looks straight at* JANETTA *and smiles.*)
DEREK: Shall we get him a suit? Dress him up like Max Miller?
IAN: I'd like that, Derek. Whatever you say.
  (DEREK *looks at him more seriously.*)
DEREK: You're not professional. You like agitation. You like all
  the running around. I don't. I like quiet. I like things to be
  quiet.

49

IAN: What do you mean by that, Derek? Quiet as the grave?
> (IAN *smiles.* DEREK *takes a quick glance around him, angry now, and moves right in towards* IAN, *his face right beside his.*)

DEREK: Learn to listen. Didn't you go to school? Didn't you go to listening class? What's wrong? Do you want me to shout in your ear?
> (DEREK's *mouth is right by* IAN's *ear.*)
>
> Keep off my patch.

IAN: Where's your patch, Derek?
> (*And now* DEREK *smiles, moving his mouth in to* IAN's *ear, like a lover.*)

DEREK: Everywhere you look. (*Then he moves away, resuming his earlier, pleasant manner.*)
> Did you hear? I bought a new house in Ruislip.
> (*He smiles at* JANETTA *again.*)
> What's clever is: from the outside my house looks like all the others. Yeah.
> (JANETTA *watches.* DEREK *is quiet again.*)
> And so do I.
> (*And suddenly, there is an unspoken signal for the whole group to break up, which it does in a series of amiable handshakes, as if it were just a party ending.*)
> Goodnight then, Ian.

IAN: Goodnight, Derek.

DEREK: I'll see you.

IAN: I'll be around.
> (DEREK *shakes* JANETTA's *hand, as he heads towards the club.*)

DEREK: Very nice to meet you. We're going this way. Goodnight. Goodnight, everyone.
> (*And the group heads off towards the club, as* IAN *puts his arm round* JANETTA *to lead her away down the alley.*)

JANETTA: (*Voice over*) The funny thing was: I felt quite lightheaded. And Ian was laughing. It meant nothing to him. We had one more night and then next day I had to go home.

57. INT. LEONARD'S ROOM. DAY

At once JANETTA *comes in through the door of their room and finds* LEONARD *sitting reading. She is carrying a small suitcase and is all benign energy.* LEONARD *turns and smiles.*

JANETTA: Hello, my dear.

LEONARD: Well, you're back.

> (*She reaches down and kisses him, then starts to take her coat off. Suzie looks up, interested.*)

> How was your aunt?

JANETTA: Actually, she was terrific. She seems to have forgiven me.

> (*She puts her arms round him from behind.*)

> I said, did it make a difference that you were a very good man?

> (*He smiles.*)

> Have you been all right?

LEONARD: Perfectly.

> (*He hasn't moved from his desk. He is quiet, as if half amused, half embarrassed.*)

> You look well.

JANETTA: Thank you, so do you.

> (*She picks up Suzie and hugs her. She sits down on the bed. There is a funny hiatus, as if neither of them knows what to say. Then, after a while, she knows she must say something.*)

> I missed you, Leonard.

LEONARD: Good, well I'm glad.

58. INT. POETRY SOCIETY. EVENING AND NIGHT

Montage. JANETTA *and* LEONARD *coming together up the stairs of the Poetry Society to be greeted at once by some members who are standing about on a first-floor landing with drinks and pipes and cigarettes already in their hands. There are about twenty of them standing about opposite large wooden doors, nearly all men.*

JANETTA: (*Voice over*) That's how it was, I'll always remember. We went out that evening. As it happened, Leonard was on wonderful form.

> (*Through the group,* CHARLIE, *the other poet, pushes through to meet* LEONARD *as he arrives. He is short, with thick black hair.*)

CHARLIE: There you are, good to see you, Leonard.

LEONARD: Hallo, Charlie.

> (LEONARD *shakes hands and greets some other poets:*)

> Hallo, Richard. Hallo, Ben.

CHARLIE: Are you nervous?

(They are moving through towards the room where the Poetry Society is held.)

LEONARD: Nervous? Why would I be nervous? The book's written . . .

(He greets a poet standing by the doorway.)

Hallo . . .

(CHARLIE and JANETTA overtake him and enter the room.)

Everything's fine.

(Now we're inside the room. LEONARD is standing at the mantelpiece talking to an attentive room, everyone ranged round in a mixture of armchairs and hard chairs, so it's half social, half formal. JANETTA discreetly to one side.)

People claim poetry doesn't *do* anything. They say, what does it get done? *(He moves forward and starts to cross the room.)* Isn't it *weak* to sit around thinking and writing when there's been so much destruction in the world? *(He pauses a second.)* I say no. It's strength. It's true strength. Truly. The hard thing is not to do, but to see. It's seeing that's hard. You get strength from looking things full in the face. Seeing everything, missing nothing, and not being frightened.

(As he speaks, he turns and looks JANETTA in the face from across the room.)

And now I'll read.

(But before he does so, we cut at once on to a group later, everyone standing around to congratulate him, JANETTA standing a little way apart, the perfectly discreet literary girlfriend.)

JANETTA: *(Voice over)* People liked his reading, I mean, it was good. And everyone enjoyed it. Looking back, he had a triumph, I'd say.

(CHARLIE comes up to him.)

CHARLIE: Well, you're pretty sly.

LEONARD: What do you mean?

CHARLIE: Writing all that lot. How long did it take?

LEONARD: Oh, not so long.

(JANETTA walks up to join them. He draws her to him, his arm round her waist, the two of them a couple.)

And Janetta was beside me.

(He looks at her a moment.)

JANETTA: *(Voice over)* Then next morning he left.

59. INT. BERYL'S STUDIO. DAY

*Beryl's surprisingly spacious studio. It is on a top floor with fine
overhead light streaming down from fanlights.* BERYL *is working on an
oil painting, which is so far only sketched in. She has a cigarette in her
mouth. Around her is evidence of multiple occupancy – a whole range of
work of which we get an unfinished impression. Everything seems to be
half finished, maquettes or abandoned canvases.*

BERYL *is working opposite a small curtained area. At the sound of*
JANETTA *coming in, she turns at once.*

BERYL: Oh, it's you.

JANETTA: Yes.

    (JANETTA *is standing at the door, unannounced. She looks pale.*)

BERYL: I thought you might visit me. Are you all right?

    (JANETTA *moves a couple of steps towards her. Now we can see
what has been hidden by the curtain – a naked male model, with
short hair, quite young and athletic. She stops.*)

    Do you know Anton?

JANETTA: No. No, I don't.

    (BERYL *gestures towards the model.*)

BERYL: I think you'd better break for five minutes. Anton.
    Janetta.

    (*She waves them together in introduction. The naked man moves
towards* JANETTA *and gravely shakes her by the hand. He sounds
Slav.*)

ANTON: How do you do?

    (*He walks away to the far end of the studio, to put one some
clothes.*)

BERYL: I got home from work. I found Leonard had left this as a
    forwarding address.

BERYL: It's not mine. I borrow it.

JANETTA: How are you? Is he here?

BERYL: He was. But he isn't.

    (*She looks at her a moment, as if deciding how much to say.*)

    I'll get you some tea.

    (BERYL *moves to the small electric ring, beside which there is a
ready-made pot of tea and a milk bottle, set among scattered
brushes and paints.*)

JANETTA: I just got this message. Leaving me the flat and saying
    . . . I don't know . . . it was time to go. Nothing more than that.

53

(BERYL *doesn't turn, just goes on pouring.*)

JANETTA: I've been up all night. I can't stop crying.

BERYL: Well then, drink this.

(*She hands her the tea, oddly matter of fact.* ANTON *is dressing at the far end of the room.*)

JANETTA: Did he talk to you?

BERYL: Briefly. He's left his job.

JANETTA: Yes. I called the BBC. It completely stunned me.

(BERYL *is watching her, not moving.* JANETTA *is hesitant.*)

What . . . I mean, did he say why? Apart from anything, why should I get the flat?

BERYL: It's a gift.

JANETTA: Yes, but it makes me feel awful. It's wrong. I can't live there without him.

BERYL: No?

(BERYL *turns back quizzically and gets herself some tea.* JANETTA *half laughs.*)

JANETTA: It would seem as if I'd just taken advantage of him.

(BERYL *looks down thoughtfully.*)

Well, I can't do it.

(*She stops, finding it hard to go on.*)

Will you tell me . . . do you know where he's gone?

(BERYL *just looks at her, then moves across the studio, nods at* ANTON *in acknowledgement as he leaves, and lights a new cigarette.*)

Look, the other thing is . . . I mean, I feel dreadful. I've got to ask you. I've been seeing someone else. Was that the reason? Honestly? Did Leonard know?

(BERYL *just watches, her expression not changing. But this time it is* JANETTA *who rushes on at once.*)

What's crazy is, I've been thinking, we discussed fidelity. He was quite clear. He said it didn't matter. He said you should never feel tied down. He said we should be free.

BERYL: What, and you believed him?

JANETTA: Yes, of course. He said it.

(BERYL *looks at her with an expression, half amusement, half contempt, as if she were finally exhausted by this* naïveté.)

Please tell me, what did he say to you?

(BERYL *looks down, having decided to stop avoiding her.*)

BERYL: Yes, he came here. He said . . .

JANETTA: What?

BERYL: I don't know. Weeks ago he'd left you some note. On your pillow.

JANETTA: Yes. I wanted to go back to the seaside.

BERYL: That's right. He knew then.

JANETTA: How?

BERYL: He just knew. (*She shrugs slightly.*) The note was his way of saying he wasn't going to stand in your way.

(JANETTA *turns away, confused.*)

JANETTA: But why? I mean, I can't believe it. For goodness' sake, that's why I asked to go. So this wouldn't happen. Why didn't he say something? It's ridiculous. Why can't people just say what they feel?

(BERYL *has already stopped listening, unimpressed. She draws at her cigarette, like a much older woman, and speaks quietly now.*)

BERYL: You should grow up.

JANETTA: Pardon?

BERYL: You're like a lot of women. People tell them it's sweet. But it isn't. Staying innocent is just a kind of cowardice.

(*She looks up from her chair now, real feeling taking over from the earlier impatience.*)

If you'd looked once . . . (*She pauses.*) If you'd looked at Leonard, I mean really looked, looked deep, you'd have understood.

(*She smiles and gets up from the chair.*)

Leonard said nothing, I'm sure. For at least two reasons. For a start, he's English. (*She stops, fighting back feeling.*) And for another he's a very nice man.

JANETTA: Oh, that!

BERYL: Yes, that!

(*There is a sudden violence between them as they are fiercely opposed, all caution gone.*)

And I mean really nice. Not fake. Not innocent. I imagine he knew who held the cards.

JANETTA: What do you mean, *cards*? It wasn't like that.

BERYL: Wasn't it?

JANETTA: No.

(BERYL *smiles, confident of her own case.*)

BERYL: Why should you be different? It's about power. You hurt him because you knew you'd get away with it. (*She nods slightly.*) You hurt him because you had nothing at risk. (JANETTA *is really hurt by this.*)

JANETTA: That isn't true.

BERYL: Oh no, I'm sure that isn't how it started. I'm sure it was fine at the beginning. It always is. The early days. Then one person notices they aren't *quite* as much in love as the other. They stop and think, 'Oh, I see, I've less to lose here . . .'
(*She stops and glares at* JANETTA.)
And that is where the inequality begins.
(*She is right by the far table again, getting another cigarette from the table piled with paints and brushes.*)
Oh, it may be terribly subtle. Because it's unspoken. It's just a shift. But it happens. And both of you know.
(*She turns back.*)
That's when you grow up. When you know you have power. And you use it deliberately for the first time.
(BERYL *smiles bitterly.* JANETTA *is nervous, defensive.*)

JANETTA: I didn't do that.

BERYL: Didn't you?
(BERYL *looks down and smiles to herself, as if it didn't matter any more.*)
I left, remember? I took my things one morning. I got out the way. Because I was powerless. (*She thinks a moment, remembering.*) I don't think he noticed.
(*There's a silence. The mood has changed decisively, now full of melancholy.*)

JANETTA: I'm sorry. I had no idea.

BERYL: No, well, you wouldn't.

JANETTA: But . . .
(*She stops.*)

BERYL: What?

JANETTA: You were always so welcoming.

BERYL: Oh, yes.

JANETTA: You told me in the bathroom that night . . .

BERYL: I did.

JANETTA: You said you and Leonard were just friends.

BERYL: So we were. Yes.

JANETTA: You said you didn't mind.
(*This time* BERYL *looks at her uncharitably.*)

BERYL: You have this habit of believing what people say. It isn't charming. It's actually horrible. Because you only do it when it suits you.
(*She gets up and moves decisively across the studio.*)
And now I think you'd better go.
(JANETTA, *taken aback by the suddenness of* BERYL's *moving, panics and raises her voice.*)
JANETTA: Where is he?
BERYL: Gone. He gave up on you.
JANETTA: I don't believe you.
BERYL: He said . . . (*She stops, checking herself.*) Leonard said, 'You never get it back. If it's perfect.'
(*She looks down and goes to the door, knowing how much she has hurt* JANETTA.)
I hope this new man makes you happy. What does he do?
JANETTA: Property.
BERYL: Good. That should suit you.
(*She pauses a moment, her hand on the door.*)
And which way is the balance this time?

60. INT. LEONARD'S ROOM. NIGHT

At once a shaft of light from the door falls across the battered face of JULIUSZ JANOWSKI. *He is lying on the bed in the little room. He has been savagely beaten. An eye is swollen and closed. There are cuts across his face. His lip is swollen, and his whole face is distorted. Blearily he tries to open an eye.* JANETTA *is standing, shocked, at the door.*
JANETTA: My god, what's happened?
(*She is about to turn on the light.*)
JULIUSZ: Don't turn on that light.
(*She pauses a moment, then closes the door. Then she moves across to a less harsh lamp on the floor, and lights it, so she can see.*)
I'm sorry. I needed to hide.
(*He makes a small effort to move. She reassures him.*)
JANETTA: It's all right.
JULIUSZ: I needed the darkness.
JANETTA: How did you get in?
JULIUSZ: I've got a key. We're your landlords. Ian bought this building last week.
(*She is still stooped on the floor, frozen in horror at his face. But*

*now she moves across to the kettle which is on the unlit gas ring by
the fire.*)

JANETTA: Here. Let me.

JULIUSZ: Please. You mustn't tell Ian. If he asks, say you haven't
seen me. If he sees me, he'll go crazy.

(JANETTA *looks up anxiously from the cupboard where she's
searching for the Dettol.*)

I know Ian. He's going to get himself killed.

(JANETTA *moves to the bed and starts to bathe his face with
cotton-wool. He winces as the Dettol stings.*)

We were pushing too hard. It's getting stupid. They let you
have some fun for a while. Then they say, 'Right. That's
your limit.'

(*As he says this, she presses the cotton-wool against his lip and he
frowns.*)

JANETTA: There.

(*He turns and tries to smile at her.*)

JULIUSZ: (*On a point of pride*) We never had people fight for us.
Never. That's the job. You expect it. We do our own
fighting.

(*She looks at his beaten face.*)

But I tell you . . . those days are gone.

(*She starts on a fresh wound.*)

Ian won't see it. You know. Well, that's Ian. He won't
accept anything. That's how he is. I'm going to miss him.

(*He takes hold of her wrist a moment, to stop her work, and looks
her in the eye. She is bent over him.*)

They beat me up in an alley. Like a pig. Like a dog. They
kicked me.

(*She holds his gaze. His eyes are moist.*)

Janetta, I'm heading home.

(*There is a moment, then she nods.*)

JANETTA: Yes.

JULIUSZ: Do you have a home?

JANETTA: Oh, yes. With five sisters. In a place we call Weston-
super-Mare.

JULIUSZ: It sounds nice.

JANETTA: It is. But I've left it. (*She pauses.*) And I think it may be
hard to go back.

(*She resumes her work.*)

58

JULIUSZ: You know you should talk to him. He worships you.

JANETTA: Does he?

JULIUSZ: Why yes. He always says . . .

(*He stops.*)

JANETTA: No, go on.

JULIUSZ: 'That woman will be really useful.' He always wanted
you should run the whole thing.

(*She smiles.*)

JANETTA: Yes.

JULIUSZ: Or rather, at least be the front for it.

(*She nods.*)

JANETTA: Yes.

JULIUSZ: He says, no one can refuse her. How do you say no to
her? (*He smiles at the neatness of it.*) No one can. And they
think, 'Hey, she's a nice person.'

(*He pauses a moment.* JANETTA *is looking at him.*)

And that is a thing we can use.

(*She looks at him, with great sadness, not moving.*)

JANETTA: Do you want to sleep, Juliusz?

JULIUSZ: Yes, I'd like to.

(*He makes a slight effort to get up again.*)

JANETTA: No, it's all right. Sleep here.

(*She puts a hand on his chest, to tell him to sleep. Then she gets
up and goes over to the cupboard where the familiar mattress is
kept. She stops short, looking at it, the emotion finally
overwhelming her.*)

There's a spare mattress. Honestly, I've done this before.

61. INT. LEONARD'S ROOM. NIGHT

Later. JANETTA *has laid the mattress, so that the two beds are side by
side, in the old way. She is in her slip, moving to get into the
improvised bed. She pulls the covers up around her. You think*
JULIUSZ *is asleep, but in the darkness he suddenly speaks.*

JULIUSZ: I mean, he likes you. He likes you as well. But also
you're useful.

(*We are now very close to* JANETTA, *who is lying her face
towards the ceiling. She replies more to herself than* JULIUSZ.)

JANETTA: I know.

59

JANETTA's *face as she walks along the street to the club. Then we see the familiar alley.* IAN *has parked his car bang in the middle and is sitting on the bonnet, writing, and all his books are around him, his office improvised in the middle of the alleyway. Around him on the pavement are his metal pails full of coins. He seems cheery and unselfconscious as* JANETTA *approaches.*

JANETTA: Ian.

IAN: Hello. How are you, gorgeous?

JANETTA: I'm fine.

> (*He has continued his work, barely stopping.*)

IAN: You haven't seen Juliusz?

JANETTA: I have.

> (IAN *looks up, interested now.*)

IAN: You have? Where is he?

JANETTA: Ian, he's on a boat. I saw him off at Victoria.

> (IAN *is bewildered by this.*)
> He's going back to Poland.

IAN: Poland? He hates bloody Poland.

> (*She moves towards him. He is still sitting on the bonnet. She puts a hand on his knee to calm him.*)

JANETTA: Ian, they beat him up.

> (IAN *looks at her.*)

IAN: How badly?

JANETTA: He was cut about the face. (*She looks down.*) He was ashamed.

IAN: What do you mean?

JANETTA: He couldn't face seeing you.

IAN: I don't believe you. Don't be ridiculous. Juliusz! He must be nuts!

JANETTA: He can't help it. Juliusz feels he's let you down.

> (IAN *looks at her, not understanding, fighting back his anger.*)
> He said, would I ask you something? He said he thought you might listen to me.

IAN: Well?

JANETTA: He said there were ten of them. All with sticks.

> (IAN *looks at her mistrustfully, knowing what's coming.*)
> Don't go after them. Ian, he made me promise. Slow up. The fun's over.

(*There is just the shadow of a reaction from* IAN *before she speaks again.*)

Ian, you told me once, you knew when to stop.

(*He looks at her again, then suddenly gets down from the car in an agony of frustration. He takes some steps along the alley. He stands like a child, overwhelmed by an emotion he can't express.*)

IAN: Jesus Christ, Janetta, this fucking city! There's nowhere. There's nowhere. It's like I'm hemmed in.

(JANETTA *looks at him, helplessly, just waiting. He starts to make a joke of it, to turn away his bitterness.*)

It's like, I tell you, I don't understand the species. I mean, by twenty-five, you can reproduce yourself. The job's done. Then what are we meant to do for the rest of our lives? Just sit around and get boring? *Just be boring?*

(JANETTA *smiles.*)

JANETTA: I believe that is what most people do.

(*He looks down, kicking his heel against the pavement, trying to calm down.*)

IAN: What can they do? I mean, they can only *kill* you. I suppose . . . was there a message? Was it Derek?

(*He turns back.*)

It's Derek, isn't it?

JANETTA: It's his men.

IAN: Did Derek say he'd kill me?

(JANETTA *does not reply.* IAN *pauses a moment.*)

He'd do it too.

JANETTA: He will.

IAN: Oh yes, I know. I don't trust anyone who likes playing golf.

(*He turns and looks at her a moment. Then moves towards her for the first time, as if to break bad news gently.*)

Janetta, you know it's going to get rough now. I think you sort of see that. I think you should probably get out the way. (*He looks down, embarrassed.*) I don't want you to, believe me. But for your own sake.

JANETTA: Of course. Yes, I knew that. (*She looks away, shaking her head slightly.*) I'll go quietly. You needn't fret.

(*He is very close to her, knowing how hurt she is, hopeless at dealing with it.*)

IAN: You can go back to your poet. Can't you? He loves you. From what I've heard. He's always been good to you. You like him, don't you?

JANETTA: Oh, yes. (*She tries to smile.*) Yes, I do.

(*They hug each other. He tries to sound more assured.*)

IAN: I think you were always with him. Really. Weren't you? You shouldn't have taken any notice of me. I used to joke. Didn't I? I was always so rude about all those types. But you're happier with them. Aren't you?

(*She doesn't reply.*)

Aren't you?

(*She still doesn't reply.*)

Janetta, please say you are.

(JANETTA *moves back from him. She looks up at him, a look we have not seen before. It's defiance, the look of someone who will not tell the other person what they want to hear. It is full of pride. Finally, he looks away.*)

JANETTA: What about you?

IAN: Oh, you know . . . it's hard for me, Janetta.

(*He smiles, apologetic.*)

It's hard to give up fighting.

(*He is suddenly quiet, thoughtful.*)

And I don't like this Derek, you know?

(*She looks at him, knowing what he will do. He smiles and then makes a gesture towards the car.*)

Tell you what, I tell you, I got hold of some petrol.

JANETTA: Yes?

IAN: Shall we go somewhere? Leave London? You and me? Do you know somewhere?

(*They both smile at the absurdity of it.*)

Somewhere we can go together?

(*She nods slightly. She hugs him.*)

JANETTA: Yes, I know where.

63. EXT. LANE. DAY

The repeated shot of the trees seen from a speeding vehicle. The music repeated from the opening shots of the film. We are looking up towards the trees, with the sun streaming through them.

JANETTA: (*Voice over*) We went to the beach. We walked together.

64. EXT. BEACH. DAY

High summer. The beach is quite busy, or at least as busy as we have seen it. Maybe thirty or forty people about. Low tide. IAN, *fully dressed for London, has taken off his shoes and socks and is walking along the water's edge with* JANETTA, *who is also shoeless. He is laughing and joking a great deal, but we don't hear him.*

JANETTA: (*Voice over*) I don't remember anything we said. Except I knew what he'd do when he got back to London. He told me. And I knew he meant it. He had no care for himself.

65. EXT. BEACH. DAY

Later. Still brilliant. Still many people about. But IAN *is sitting with his legs tucked up in front of him, looking out to sea.* JANETTA *is sitting also, to one side and behind him, so she can only see the side of his face. He is lost in thought. We see him from her point of view.*

JANETTA: (*Voice over*) And it's true. I never heard from him again. When Rachman was all over the papers, I remember I searched for Ian's name.
  (*He turns a moment, and smiles absently at her, still wrapped in his own thoughts.*)
  But it wasn't there. He was one of so many. And I'm sure he was quickly swept out the way.

66. EXT. BEACH. EVENING

The water at sunset. Nobody about now. Just a still ocean, with the sun setting gloriously on the horizon. No one and nothing in view.

JANETTA: (*Voice over*) When evening came, we went in the water.
  (*Now the dunes, in the dying light. The green tufts standing out against the fading horizon. Again, deserted, no one seen.*)
  Then, alone, made love in the dunes.
  (*A moment, then fade to black. A few seconds darkness, then:*)

67. EXT. BEACH. DAY

We fade up on the same scene forty years later. The whole beach has been built over. We are no longer looking at dunes, but at rows of bungalows and semi-detached houses in the regular post-war style.

JANETTA: (*Voice over*) These places are gone now. Last year I
went down to the sea. It was bricked over. The bay has gone.
England's bricked over. Just like Ian always said it would
be . . .

68. EXT. STREETS. DAY

*We begin to travel now along the front of the South Coast, along
endless rows of Acacia Avenues, identical houses replacing identical
houses, all going by from a speeding vehicle.*
JANETTA: (*Voice over*) There used to be spaces. You took them for
granted. In England, there were views. Everywhere you
turned, you saw countryside, stretching away and
beyond . . .
(*We turn a corner. Beyond this row of houses, another row.
Beyond that, another.*)
Now the South Coast of England is one long stretch of
bricked-in dormitory town.

69. INT. LIBRARY. DAY/NIGHT. MONTAGE

Back into 1948. We are back in the foyer of the library. JANETTA
*now sits behind a separate desk at the library, supervising the whole
work of the lending part. She is not much older in her looks but her
clothes are smarter and more formal.*
JANETTA: (*Voice over*) I resumed life. I went back to the library.
For years I worked as if in a dream.
(JANETTA, *behind her new mask of respectability, goes to help a
customer, her walk assured, her manner easy.*)
Later, I married. Then my husband died, very young, of
cancer.
(*Alone, she leaves the library at night, turning out all the lights
one by one.*)
I mean no disrespect to his memory when I say, thirty years
later, his death affects me less than the events I have
described.
(*The huge foyer of the library is suddenly in darkness.*)
It was as if I were numb, my feelings long locked inside me.
And they could not be released.

70. EXT. STREET. NIGHT

At night JANETTA *walks home alone through London's empty streets, in the sculptured clothes of her later years.*

JANETTA: (*Voice over*) I knew what I'd done. I had no illusions. All the time I had my reasons. But that is not always enough. (*She reaches for the key to go into her home.*)

71. INT. FLAT. NIGHT/DAY

At once the memory returns of LEONARD *sitting at the desk writing.*

JANETTA: (*Voice over*) I loved Leonard. I knew I loved Leonard. I knew I had loved him all along.
(*Now, the memory of him reaching for his hat as he goes to the door and goes out.*)
I understand to this day that people like Leonard do not speak their feelings. But I still to this day am not wholly sure why.

72. EXT. ROAD. DAY

The memory of the road, the sun flashing through the trees, the same bend in the lane we have seen before.

JANETTA: (*Voice over*) I have one concern only . . .

73. INT./EXT. MONTAGE. DAY/NIGHT

A montage of memories, starting with JANETTA *at the door, coming in to greet* LEONARD, *who is at his desk.* JANETTA *putting her arms round him to kiss him. Silent, no sound. At the other side of the room Suzie jumps from the table to the sofa.*

JANETTA: (*Voice over*) At a level below understanding, below instinct even, I cannot control a certain trick of the mind which tells me: 'This is not it . . .'
(IAN, *now, on the telephone at the Empire Club, seen from across the smoky, crowded room, gesticulating to an unseen second party. Noiseless, silent.*)
'This is not the only chance you get at living your life . . .'
(JULIUSZ *being kicked like a dog by a group of men in a dark alley. He is crouched over on the ground, curled up, as men take*

turns to kick him in the stomach. We see this from a distance.
Noiseless, silent. Then:)
It's an illusion, I see that, like a flaw in my computer. A voice
keeps telling me, I get a second chance . . .
(*The side of* IAN's *face as he sits on the beach again, staring out
to sea.*)
'This is not it,' it says, over and over. But it is.
(JANETTA's *face as she sits, watching* IAN.)
Of that I am sure.

74. EXT. MONTAGE. EVENING

*Now again silently, the bungalows speeding by, faster and faster, in
endless, identical succession.*
JANETTA: (*Voice over*) These events, I suppose, detain me and me
only. No one else remembers them, or if they do, then quite
differently. To them, they yield a different meaning.
(*The bungalows cross-fade now, and become dunes, the sand and
green grass going by at the same speed.*)
I remember them as if they were yesterday . . .
(*We turn and head out at high speed across the sea, skimming,
like a low bird, just above the level of the water.*)
But of course I shall not remember them for long.
(*Fade to black.*)

WETHERBY

The première of *Wetherby*, a Greenpoint Film presented by Film Four International and Zenith Productions, took place at the Curzon West End, London, on 8 March 1985. The cast included:

JEAN TRAVERS	Vanessa Redgrave
MARCIA PILBOROUGH	Judi Dench
JOHN MORGAN	Tim McInnerny
STANLEY PILBOROUGH	Ian Holm
MIKE LANGDON	Stuart Wilson
KAREN CREASY	Suzanna Hamilton

Other parts were played as follows:

The Wetherby characters

VERITY BRAITHWAITE	Majorie Yates
ROGER BRAITHWAITE	Tom Wilkinson
CHRISSIE	Penny Downie
LANDLADY	Brenda Hall
LILLY	Marjorie Sudell
DEREK, CHRISSIE'S HUSBAND	Patrick Blackwell

In the past

YOUNG JEAN TRAVERS	Joely Richardson
JIM MORTIMER	Robert Hines
YOUNG MARCIA	Katy Behean
MR MORTIMER	Bert King
MRS MORTIMER	Paula Tilbrook
ARTHUR	Christopher Fulford
YOUNG MALAY	David Foreman

The school

SUZIE BANNERMAN	Stephanie Noblett
SIR THOMAS	Richard Marris
BOATMAN	Jonathan Lazenby
FIRST PAGE	Nigel Rooke
SECOND PAGE	John Robert

DRAMA TEACHER	Norman Mills
PRETENTIOUS PARENTS	{ Vanessa Rosenthal Trevor Lunn
MR VARLEY	Guy Nicholls
NEUROTIC TEACHER	Ian Bleasdale
HELPFUL PARENT	Peter Martin
MISS TRAVERS'S CLASS	{ Mouth, Dave, Dob, Flash, Jonny, Lebanon, Tracey, Bez, Jen, Jessica, Rhianon, Maddy, Paul, Toby, Marcus, Masher, Andy, Janet, Peter, Ram, Liz, Ed, Suzanne, Lesley, Shaun

The police

POLICEWOMAN	Diane Whitley
CID POLICEMAN	Mike Kelly
POLICEMAN	Howard Crossley
RANDALL, THE POLICE DOCTOR	Matthew Guinness
POLICE SERGEANT	Ted Beyer

Director	David Hare
Producer	Simon Relph
Associate Producer	Patsy Pollock
Music	Nick Bicât
Designer	Hayden Griffin
Director of photography	Stuart Harris
Costume designers	Jane Greenwood
	Lindy Hemming
Editor	Chris Wimble

NOTE

The script as published does not correspond exactly to the final version of the film. In the editing I changed round a few scenes which I have here retained in an order which makes them easier to read.

D.H.

1. CREDITS

Under the credits the sound of a conversation slowly drifts in, and then under it is established the sound of a crowded place. Their talk overlaps.

JEAN: (*Voice over*) Nixon? Yes.

STANLEY: (*Voice over*) Yes? You remember.

JEAN: (*Voice over*) Of course I remember.

STANLEY: (*Voice over*) It's funny how many people forget.

JEAN: (*Voice over*) Nobody forgets Nixon. And it wasn't so long ago.

STANLEY: (*Voice over*) Ten years.

JEAN: (*Voice over*) Already? My God.

STANLEY: (*Voice over*) What was happening in Wetherby ten years ago?
(*A silence.*)
He was a distinguished member of my own profession.

JEAN: (*Voice over*) What? Liar?

STANLEY: (*Voice over*) No, not liar. Solicitor. Well, lawyer. He trained as a lawyer.

JEAN: (*Voice over*) Liar or lawyer?

STANLEY: (*Voice over*) Is there a difference? I wonder, have you got time for another drink?

2. INT. PUB. DAY

Continuation. There is a sudden silence, and the picture arrives. In intense close-up. We are looking at JEAN, *a thin woman with grey hair, in her late forties. A cigarette burns in front of her. Across from her is* STANLEY, *a rumpled, baggy, instantly likeable figure in a sports jacket with a check shirt and a tie. Through an archway at the back of the shot we can detect that we are in a pub. Light falls sideways, in great shafts, into the bar. But we are in the deserted restaurant.*

STANLEY: Wouldn't it be marvellous if Nixon walked in now? Right now. You just can't help it, it would cheer everyone up. (*He laughs. At the door of the pub a dog scampers in and is chased out.* FARMERS *stand drinking at the bar in wellington boots.*)

JEAN: Oh God, Stanley, you and I have lived in this town for too long.

(STANLEY *looks at her, then he looks down. There is a sudden seriousness in his manner.* JEAN *looks away, then he shrugs.*)
You know the best thing about Nixon, I'll tell you . . .
STANLEY: Shouldn't you be getting back to school?
JEAN: No, listen, I'll tell you. The one Nixon story, all right?
(*There is a call of 'Time, gentlemen, please' in the main bar, but* JEAN *is leaning forward, intent.*)
When he first met Pat, she didn't like him very much. So, after a bit, she said she didn't want to go out with him any more. 'Well,' he said, 'it breaks my heart, Pat, and I'll only stop dating you on one condition.' And she said, 'What's that?' 'That I can always be the chauffeur.' So when she went out with other men, to the cinema, say, Nixon would drive them. He'd drive them to the cinema, they'd get out, they'd go in, her and her date, and Nixon would *wait outside*. He'd wait outside during the whole film with a packet of popcorn or a piece of chewing-gum. Then out they'd come and he'd drive them home. Now . . . I ask you . . . what does that tell you about Nixon?
(STANLEY *smiles.*)
STANLEY: Jean . . . I ask you . . . what does it tell you about Pat?

3. EXT. JEAN'S HOUSE. NIGHT

A perfect Yorkshire farmhouse, rather dilapidated, set in the crook of a hill. Lights burning at its windows. Outside, a wild but tended garden. Old garden furniture, abandoned bicycles. An image of run-down serenity.

4. INT. JEAN'S HOUSE. NIGHT

Inside there is a dinner party going on at a big wooden table which is at the centre of the kitchen cum dining room which takes up most of the farmhouse's ground floor. Everyone at the table, save one person, is in their late forties or early fifties. They are all at their ease, with the dimmed lights, the emptied casserole dish, the green salad and cheese, the very many bottles of red and white wine.
JEAN: If you want to be loved in life, there's no use in having opinions.
VERITY: I think you're right.

JEAN: Who loves people who have opinions? The people who get loved are the people who are easy. Easy to get along with.

ROGER: Jean . . .

STANLEY: Have we lost the corkscrew? I can't do the bloody thing.

(STANLEY *is standing hopelessly trying to open another bottle of wine.* ROGER *and* VERITY *are looking at each other in the meaningful way of couples at dinner parties.* ROGER *is a pedantic, meticulous man in his forties, in grey flannels and a sports jacket.* VERITY *is a forthright woman, slightly overdressed for the occasion, a natural member of the Geoffrey Boycott supporters' club.* MARCIA *is a warm and funny woman in her forties, naturally good-humoured and outgoing, a touch insensitive. She has taken up* JEAN'S *point at the other end of the table.*)

MARCIA: There's a new girl at work, at the library, the sort of girl men fall for, vacant . . .

JEAN: Cool.

MARCIA: Distant, that's right. She doesn't really have a personality, she just has a way of suggesting to men that she'll be whatever they want her to be. Not a *person*, not a real person . . .

(ROGER *smiles, easy, thinking he understands.*)

ROGER: What's she done, this girl?

MARCIA: Well, I'll tell you . . .

ROGER: Just *been* this thing you object to, or has she done anything wrong yet?

MARCIA: She exists.

MORGAN: She's young.

(*This is the first time* MORGAN *has spoken. He sits, younger and less drunk than the others. He is only twenty-five, in corduroys. He is heavy, self-contained, slow.*)

MARCIA: Yes, if you like. She's young. So . . .

MORGAN: It's an offence.

MARCIA: But there's no . . . (*As she searches for the word, she becomes suddenly passionate*) her . . . nothing which is her. I look at the young – truly – and I am mystified. Want nothing. Need nothing. Have no ambitions. Get married, have children, get a mortage. A hundred thousand years of human evolution, brontosaurus, tyrannosaurus, man. And

73

the sum ambition? Two-up two-down in the West Riding of
Yorkshire, on a custom-built estate of brick and glass.
(*Addressing the whole table, which is now stilled*) That isn't
right, is it? Can anyone tell me?
(ROGER *smiles, still cool.*)
ROGER: She's young. That's all you're saying. She's young.
(*At once a large drop of water splashes on the table from the
ceiling, right in front of him.* JEAN *giggles and looks up.*)
JEAN: Oh God.

5. INT. LANDING. NIGHT

MORGAN, *with a torch, coming down the stepladder that leads to the
attic.* JEAN *is watching from the landing. The sound of the dinner
going on in the distance.* MORGAN *stops on the ladder.*
MORGAN: I think it's fixed.
JEAN: Thank you.
(MORGAN *is still a moment.*)
A slate fell in the night. I was frightened to go up there.
MORGAN: It's all right.
(*He stands quite still on the ladder.*)
Shall we go down?

6. INT. CORRIDOR. NIGHT

JEAN *moving very quickly now along the darkened corridor that leads
to the dining room from the bottom of the stairs.* MORGAN, *by contrast,
comes much more slowly, dawdling slightly on the stairs.*

7. INT. LIVING ROOM. NIGHT

JEAN *comes out of the darkness and into the dinner party. She is now
wearing grey flannel trousers. She walks past the chattering table and
goes to get coffee from the stove.* MORGAN *slips back quietly to his
place.* ROGER *looks across to where* JEAN *is now standing. He looks at
her a moment, thoughtfully.*

8. INT. SCHOOL. DAY

A bright and cheerful nineteenth-century schoolroom. Wooden desks and chairs in deep brown. JEAN *standing, addressing a mixed-sex class, very attentive. They are all about sixteen.*

JEAN: Whether our faces show. This is the question.

> (*Pause. There is a moment for them to think about it.*)
>
> We read a face. We look at a face, let's say, and into that face all sorts of things we claim to read. Mary here . . .
>
> (*We look at a girl in the front row.*)
>
> Or John . . .
>
> (*We look at* JOHN. *Earnest, with ears that stick out and low eyebrows.*)
>
> . . . whose face is sly. His face is sly. His features are sly. Is John a sly boy?

BOY: He's sly all right.

JOHN: I'm not a sly boy.

> (*The children all laugh or smile.* JOHN *smiles too.*)

JEAN: Do we become the way we look? Or do we look the way we really are?

> (*We look at* SUZIE BANNERMAN, *a girl sitting at the back. She is fresh-faced, very attractive and assured. She is fifteen. The bell rings.*)
>
> Right, everyone, that's it. That was meant to be English.
>
> (*The class begins to talk and leave. But we stay on* SUZIE. *She gets up and starts to walk down to* JEAN *at the front.* JEAN *is murmuring to herself:*)
>
> 'There's no art . . . to find the mind's construction in the face . . .'

SUZIE: Miss Travers? I wondered . . . do you have time for a chat?

9. INT. CLASSROOM. DAY

SUZIE *and* JEAN *are sitting opposite each other in the now deserted classroom. They are both at school desks.*

SUZIE: Miss Travers, do you think there's any point in my going on in the sixth form?

JEAN: Of course. Don't be silly. What makes you say that?

SUZIE: Well, it's just . . . whatever you do, you seem to end up unemployed.

JEAN: Not everyone. But I do know what you mean.

SUZIE: You get a university degree, like in French, then what?

Maybe you get to be a secretary. And that's if you're lucky. Honestly, I have really thought about it. I don't really think it's worth it, you see.

JEAN: That's not what education is, though, Suzie. If you're always thinking, I must *use* my education for a career, then you're already thinking about education in the wrong way.
Education is a thing in itself, a way of fulfilling your potential, of looking for ways of thinking, ways, which, if you're lucky, will help you not just in your career, but in your whole life.

SUZIE: What ways?

JEAN: Well, ways of being ordered, I suppose. Having some discipline in the way you think. Not always being bull-headed, learning not to rush into things.

SUZIE: Do you think uneducated people do that?

JEAN: Well, I don't. No, not necessarily. I mean, sometimes.

SUZIE: Are they inferior for not knowing how to think?

JEAN: No, of course not.

(JEAN *smiles, on the spot.* SUZIE's *questions have no side.*)

SUZIE: But if you have something . . . what you call a way of thinking, which they don't, surely you're saying you're superior?

JEAN: No, Suzie, of course I wouldn't say that.

SUZIE: What then?

JEAN: Different.

SUZIE: Better or worse?

10. EXT./INT. JEAN'S HOUSE. DAY

Jean's house from outside in the early evening sunshine. JEAN *is working, correcting exercise books. We hold the shot, as if seeing it from someone's point of view. Now* JEAN *looks up from her work and finds* MORGAN *standing there. She is at once tense. He is holding a brace of pheasant.*

MORGAN: I brought you some pheasant.

(*She doesn't move. She just stares at him.*)

Am I disturbing you?

JEAN: No.

(*She takes the schoolbooks she is correcting and closes them, then puts them in a neat pile on the table. She lines her pencil up beside them. Then she gets up.*)

Come in. I'll make you some tea.
(*She goes into the kitchen.*)

11. INT. KITCHEN. DAY

JEAN *goes across to the stove. She fills the kettle and puts it on the Aga. It is as if she is relieved to have something to do. He moves across to the table, and puts the pheasants down. Then he lifts the corner of the schoolbooks, as if to look inside the top one. There is a silence, as she looks out the window.*

JEAN: I love the slow evenings, once the summer begins to come. It doesn't get dark until eight.
   (MORGAN *watches her. She turns, smiling.*)
   Are you staying with Marcia long?
MORGAN: No. I don't know Marcia.
JEAN: What? (*Looking amazed*) But you said . . .
MORGAN: What?
JEAN: When you came to dinner . . .
MORGAN: I met her on the doorstep.
JEAN: Who invited you?
MORGAN: No one.
   (JEAN *almost begins to laugh.*)
JEAN: What are you . . . what . . . are you saying? I don't believe this. Are you saying . . . ?

12. INT. JEAN'S HOUSE. NIGHT

Flashback. We see from inside the house as the small group of people arrives together at the door. MARCIA *and* STANLEY *are greeting* JEAN. *Then* MARCIA *introduces* MORGAN *to* JEAN.
MORGAN: (*Voice over*) I met Marcia on the doorstep, I introduced myself.

13. INT. JEAN'S HOUSE. DAY

The present. JEAN *is looking at* MORGAN, *amazed.*
JEAN: I thought you came with *her*.
MORGAN: No.
   (*A pause.*)
JEAN: It's not possible.

14. INT. JEAN'S HOUSE. NIGHT

Flashback. We return to the scene as JEAN *reaches out her hand to greet* MORGAN. MARCIA *is already going on ahead into the house.* STANLEY *is behind.*

MORGAN: (*Voice over*) Then I said 'John Morgan' and you shook my hand.

JEAN: (*Voice over*) Yes.

  (*We catch* JEAN'S *response to the handshake.*)

  Ah, hello, hello. You brought an extra.

  (*But* MARCIA *has already gone into the house, not hearing this.*)

15. INT. JEAN'S HOUSE. DAY

The present. MORGAN *and* JEAN *are now staring at each other.* MORGAN *speaks quietly.*

MORGAN: And you accepted me.

16. INT. JEAN'S HOUSE. NIGHT

Flashback. JEAN *moves round the warm, candlelit table, laying some knives and forks by the already set places.* ROGER *and* VERITY *are in nearby armchairs.*

JEAN: I'll lay an extra place.

  (*She looks across.* MORGAN *smiles.*)

MORGAN: Thank you.

17. INT. JEAN'S HOUSE. DAY

The present. JEAN *is staring at him, a more serious worry now in her voice.*

JEAN: Absurd! It's impossible!

MORGAN: No.

  (*He looks at her a moment, then takes a revolver out of his pocket and puts the end of it in his mouth. He blows his brains out. His skull explodes across the room.*)

18. EXT. JEAN'S HOUSE. DAY

Briefly, Jean's house seen from outside. The sound of a great cry from inside.

JEAN: (*Out of vision*) No! No!

19. INT. AIRPLANE. NIGHT

At once flashback to 1953. We are inside a troop carrier. Rugs are laid out on the floor. The airplane is darkened, silent, but for the two people making love, naked on the floor. The YOUNG JEAN TRAVERS *is stretched out, her head against the metal.* JIM *is twenty-two, passionate. They are both sweating. We watch them, close in.*
YOUNG JEAN: Yes! Yes!
JIM: No! Don't let me . . . no!
YOUNG JEAN: Yes!
JIM: No!
YOUNG JEAN: No, you mean, yes . . .
JIM: I mean yes. Yes!

20. EXT. AIRFIELD. NIGHT

Flashback, 1953. The darkened airfield. A wide flat space. The windsock billowing in the night. Beyond, the great hangar. The moon.

21. INT. AIRPLANE. NIGHT

Flashback, 1953. In the plane, they are now lying in each other's arms. A rug covers them.
YOUNG JEAN: Let me see . . . let me look at you.
     (*She lifts the rug to look at his naked body. Then she lifts her head and looks him full in the face.*)

22. INT. AIRPLANE. NIGHT

Later. YOUNG JEAN *is sitting along the side of the plane. She has a blanket wrapped round her. She is on the benches where the troops sit to be flown out. She has a pack of cigarettes and a lighter. She lights a cigarette.*
JIM: You're not meant to.
YOUNG JEAN: I know.
     (*In the cockpit* JIM *sits naked in the pilot's seat.*)
     Do you fly these?
JIM: Not a chance. Engine fitters don't get to fly. It's three years

before you get to go on a flying course. Longer, maybe. And then not one of these.

YOUNG JEAN: Really?

JIM: They take the troops out in these. To the jungle.

YOUNG JEAN: Ah.

JIM: To the war. You come down seven times before you get to Malaya. It takes over a week. By the time you get there, you know you've been travelling.

YOUNG JEAN: I'm sure. (*A pause.*) Did you know . . . did you realize you might have to fight when you joined?

JIM: You're an airman, you want to fly. You're a soldier, you want to fight. Not much point else.

YOUNG JEAN: No.

JIM: I'll walk you home.

23. EXT. AIRFIELD. NIGHT

Flashback, 1953. JIM *shooting the bolt on the outside of the door. He shoots another. Then a padlock, which clicks. He turns and smiles at* YOUNG JEAN *who is standing nervously on one side. They are dwarfed by the enormous tin wall of the hangar. They begin to walk along the tarmac path. As they pass the mess, we see in the steamed-up windows to a brightly lit room full of airmen, drinking and singing. As they are about to pass, the door bursts open, and crashing through comes an* AIRMAN, *who falls to the ground, followed by others, all holding pints.*

AIRMEN: Make him drink it! Make him drink it!

(*The* AIRMAN *on the ground protests. Instinctively* JIM *reaches for* JEAN, *touching her arm, covering her.*)

YOUNG JEAN: It's all right.

(*They pass on. The* AIRMEN *become distant figures, forcing drink down the man's throat as he lies on the ground. Noises of protest and excitement, tiny figures in the vast night.*)

24. EXT. VILLAGE. NIGHT

Later. JIM *and* YOUNG JEAN *walk through the village, which has a thirties feel to it – redbrick, suburban. Lampposts. A car or two.*

JIM: Happen if I were killed, I'd still say, fine. I joined to fight. Didn't have to. Could just have done National Service,

tramped the parade ground. And we're not even at war.
Well, not properly at war. Half a war. Malaya's half a war.
(*Smiles.*) But I liked the idea.
(*They stop by Jean's house. A semi in the style of all the others. A light is on upstairs.*)
Is your mum in bed?

YOUNG JEAN: I think so. (*Puts a hand on his chest, flat, just touching the material.*) If she ever asks, we saw *The Third Man*.

25. INT. HOUSE. NIGHT

Flashback, 1953. YOUNG JEAN *standing at the bottom of the stairs, looking up, listening. Then she goes into the small fifties kitchen. There is a larder, she reaches for a piece of cheese wrapped in greaseproof paper. She goes upstairs. On the landing she pauses, as she goes to the door of her room. She calls to her* MOTHER, *unseen, in the other bedroom.*

YOUNG JEAN: Still awake?

JEAN'S MOTHER: (*From her bedroom*) Yes. How was it?

YOUNG JEAN: Good.

26. INT. JEAN'S ROOM. NIGHT

YOUNG JEAN *turns on the light in her room. It is the plainest lower-middle-class bedroom. Simple desk, bed, chair. The desk is covered with books and papers. It is clear she is studying for an exam. She looks ruefully at the empty room. Then she calls:*

YOUNG JEAN: Orson Wells killed all these children, but then they shot him in a sewer in the end.
    (*A pause.*)

JEAN'S MOTHER: (*From her bedroom*) That's good.

YOUNG JEAN: Yes. Good night.

27. INT. JEAN'S ROOM. NIGHT

A little later. We look at the top of the desk. The piece of cheese is sweating in its greaseproof paper. The surface of the desk is covered with exercise books. YOUNG JEAN's *hand as she pushes a couple of books aside. Underneath, a black diary with a clasp, which she opens.*

Good, neat handwriting. She takes a pen, about to make an entry.
YOUNG JEAN: Never dreamt, never thought any such happiness
  possible. Hiding in the dark, loving a man in the dark.
  (*Although she is very quiet, she now makes a small eye movement
  in the direction of her mother's room. Her pen is poised.*)
  Never knew any such happiness possible at all.

28. EXT. LANE. EVENING

*The present. A single police car travelling along a country lane. Like a
mirage, silent, serene.*

29. EXT. JEAN'S HOUSE. EVENING

*The police car coming up the short drive to the house. Outside there are
three or four other police cars and an ambulance. The car gets near and
stops.* MIKE LANGDON *gets out. He is almost forty, with a
moustache. He is in plain clothes. He looks towards the door where a*
WORKMAN *is taking a lock off the door and putting a new one on. As*
LANGDON *moves towards the door he pauses a moment, taking in his
breath. As he does, he catches the eye of a young* POLICEWOMAN, *a
sharp-featured blonde girl of about twenty-three.*
LANGDON: How bad is it?
  (*The* POLICEWOMAN *doesn't reply.*)

30. INT. JEAN'S HOUSE. EVENING

LANGDON *comes into the room where four or five people are working
in silence, clearing up all the furniture which has had to be moved.*
MORGAN's *body is still there. A* POLICE DOCTOR *is examining it. A*
POLICEMAN *in uniform unwraps a piece of lint and shows* LANGDON
the gun. LANGDON *nods. Then the* POLICEMAN *takes it away and
almost at once from the other side another* POLICEMAN *holds up a
plain snap of* JOHN MORGAN. *It is the simplest student mugshot.*
LANGDON: Why did he do it?
POLICEMAN: Depressed, I suppose.
LANGDON: Why did he do it in here?

31. INT. JEAN'S HOUSE. EVENING

The room much quieter now. Only the sharp-featured POLICEWOMAN *stands where Jean stood earlier. A* YOUNG POLICEMAN *sits where Morgan once was. By the wall, a group of* UNIFORMED POLICEMEN *and a* POLICE PHOTOGRAPHER, *watching with* LANGDON. *The* POLICEWOMAN *stares out the window.*

POLICEWOMAN: 'I love the warm evening.' Something. Tea.
    (*Reaches for the teapot.*) 'It doesn't get dark until eight.'
    (*Turns and faces the* YOUNG POLICEMAN.) 'How long are you
    staying with Marcia?'

YOUNG POLICEMAN: 'I'm not.'

POLICEWOMAN: Shock. Move towards him. (*She does.*) 'What
    d'you mean?'

YOUNG POLICEMAN: He explains.

POLICEWOMAN: 'Unbelievable!'
    (*The* YOUNG POLICEMAN *reaches into his right pocket.*)

YOUNG POLICEMAN: Right pocket.
    (*He mimes getting a gun out. He then sticks the two fingers of his
    hand into his mouth.* MIKE LANGDON *watching this. Then the*
    YOUNG POLICEMAN *and the* POLICEWOMAN *both look to the
    floor.*)
    That's it.

32. EXT. GARDEN. NIGHT

MIKE LANGDON *sits alone now in the deserted garden of Jean's
house. He is stretched out in a chair, looking to the house. He is
thinking. Then he gets up and goes back in.*

33. JEAN'S HOUSE. NIGHT

LANGDON *walks along the side of the kitchen, running his hand along
the surface, thinking. The neat range of objects: the herbs, the olive
oil, the garlic. The cookbook open at 'Coq au vin'. Still thinking, he
moves towards the other part of the room. On the mantelpiece, an
invitation to a local amateur dramatic society. A school photo of
Jean's class. A photo of the house. A couple of candlesticks. A photo
of Jean as a young girl, standing beside the young Marcia. He reaches
towards it.*

JEAN: There seems little point . . .

(LANGDON *reacts sharply, as in guilt.* JEAN *has come into the room from the hallway and is standing in the door. She looks gaunt.*)

LANGDON: My goodness, I'm sorry, you startled me.

(JEAN *nods at the new lock on the door, where it is gleaming conspicuously. She goes over to it.*)

JEAN: The new lock. The chances of the same thing happening twice. (*Turns and looks at him.*) And anyway I let him in.

(LANGDON *looks across the room at her.*)

Doesn't matter how well locked up you are, at times you're always going to have to let people in.

(*She looks at him a moment, then crosses the room and stoops down below him to switch on the electric fire.*)

LANGDON: Are you all right?

JEAN: Yes. I've been trying to sleep. As best I may.

(JEAN *stops involuntarily, seeing something we do not see.*)

LANGDON: Oh yes, I'm sorry. We don't clean up afterwards. We just take the body away. It seems a bit callous, I know. But the thinking is if we always had to clear up, the police would spend their whole life on their knees.

(*Pause.*)

JEAN: How are you getting on?

LANGDON: Well, we have something.

(*He moves away, the photo of Jean and Marcia still in his hand.*)

He was a student.

JEAN: I see.

LANGDON: Working for his doctorate at the University of Essex. He came to the town a few days ago and rented a room.

JEAN: Are you a graduate yourself?

LANGDON: Yes. A subject of much mirth. A graduate policeman. (*Smiles, waiting to see what her reaction will be.*) This man wasn't my generation. He was younger, he was only twenty-five. He came to research at the British Library down the road.

(JEAN *has sat down.* LANGDON *looks at her a moment.*)

A blankness. A central disfiguring blankness. That's what people who knew him describe.

(JEAN *nods slightly.*)

84

JEAN: Yes . . . it's true . . . I've been trying to remember. At dinner he said so little. Until late in the evening. He seemed already set on a path. (*Smiles.*) It's funny, I mean, looking back, I took his being there for granted. Even now it doesn't seem odd.

LANGDON: Well, that's right, I've often been out to dinner, and not been quite sure who somebody was.

JEAN: No.

LANGDON: Quite.

(*There's a pause.*)

Though usually it's different if you're the hostess.

(*He waits for the reaction. But she says nothing.*)

Anyway, it turns out it wasn't completely out of the blue. The day before he'd seen Marcia Pilborough. As you know, she works at the library . . .

JEAN: Oh, I see.

LANGDON: . . . and he'd gone up to her, they'd had a conversation. He wanted to borrow a book. Afterwards we think he probably waited and started to follow her.

JEAN: Ah, well. Yes. It begins to make sense.

(LANGDON *looks at her a little nervously.*)

LANGDON: Would you say . . . I mean these things are very difficult . . . would you say that Marcia was in any way a woman who was likely to have been deliberately provocative? I mean, is lying and brought him to dinner deliberately? Or as a joke?

(*For the first time* JEAN *smiles very slightly.*)

JEAN: I don't want to be rude about Marcia – she's my best friend – but I'm afraid I don't think that possible at all.

34. EXT. RIVERSIDE. DAY

At once flashback (1953) to the sound of two girls as they walk together along a riverside, densely vegetated, the river running silver in the sun beside them. YOUNG MARCIA *is plump, likeable, unpretentious. Her hair is permed.* YOUNG JEAN *walks beside her with a garland of daisies in her hand.*

YOUNG JEAN: And London, tell me, what would that be like?

YOUNG MARCIA: London? Oh, wonderful, London would be wonderful. Just totally different. Not like Wetherby in any way.

(JEAN *puts the garland on* MARCIA's *head.* MARCIA *laughs. They embrace.*)

YOUNG JEAN: Hold on, look, you look lovely.

YOUNG MARCIA: Really?

YOUNG JEAN: Yes.

YOUNG MARCIA: I can't go back into town like this.

YOUNG JEAN: Why not?

(*They smile and carry on walking.*)

YOUNG MARCIA: It's so exciting, the idea of living in a great city. People say, oh, cities are so anonymous. But that's what's so good about them. Nobody knows who you are.

(*JEAN takes a sideways glance at her.*)

YOUNG JEAN: Marcia . . .

YOUNG MARCIA: Don't you long to get out?

YOUNG JEAN: Marcia, I'm . . .

YOUNG MARCIA: What?

YOUNG JEAN: I'm seeing an airman.

YOUNG MARCIA: Cripes! Are you serious? Does your mum know?

(*JEAN looks down.*)

I'm seeing a soldier.

(*They burst out laughing.*)

Well, what on earth are we all meant to do?

35. INT. JEAN'S HOUSE. NIGHT

Flashback. The dinner party. The two women, MARCIA and JEAN, are embracing by the stove – thirty years on from the previous scene. Behind them, people are talking. JEAN has a glossy photo in her hand.

JEAN: Oh, Marcia, thank you.

MARCIA: I knew you'd like it.

JEAN: When did you take it?

(*She holds it up. A picture of the house. Still, unchanging, beautiful.*)

My house.

(*She moves across to the table where the guests are beginning to sit down. STANLEY is in the middle of the room, looking round.*)

Look, everyone, what Marcia's brought me. A picture of the house. Do you like it?

(*For the first time in this sequence we see MORGAN. He is now sitting at the edge of the room, all by himself.*)

MORGAN: It's great.

86

(JEAN *looks at him a moment, struck by his tone.*)

36. INT. JEAN'S ROOM. NIGHT

Flashback, 1953. The YOUNG JEAN *making love to* JIM. *He is pressing her against the wall. She has her legs up around him. She is laughing. A single light is on at the desk, her books and papers lit.*
YOUNG JEAN: Jim, no, don't, for goodness' sake . . .
(*He presses further into her.*)
Goodness . . .
(*She laughs.*)
JIM: Is this a party wall?
(*He presses twice more. Peals of laughter. She takes his head into her hands.*)
YOUNG JEAN: Jim.
JIM: What?
YOUNG JEAN: Please, it's undignified.
JIM: Unladylike.
(*They smile. Very fond of each other.*)
YOUNG JEAN: Yes.
(*The sound of a door opening downstairs. A key in the latch, the front door opening.*)
Jim, oh Lord, it's my mother.
JIM: What?
YOUNG JEAN: Let me down.
(*He looks at her, presses her harder against the wall, holding her there, with his hands pressed against the wall.*)
JIM: (*Quietly*) I want to make love to you.
YOUNG JEAN: Jim . . .
(*We are in very close. First on* JEAN, *then on* JIM *as they look at each other without moving. There is a long stillness. Then the sound of lights being turned on downstairs. Then off. A creak on the stairs. Then movement, we stay on their faces.* JEAN'S MOTHER *calls from outside.*)
JEAN'S MOTHER: Jean, are you home?
YOUNG JEAN: I'm home.
JEAN'S MOTHER: Is there anything you need?
YOUNG JEAN: No, no, I'm fine.
(*There is a silence, then the sound of another door opening and a light switch. The door closes.* JIM's *face as he looks at* JEAN, *both*

87

way above the situation, heightened, in love. JEAN's *face. A slow cross-fade to:*)

37. INT. KITCHEN. NIGHT

The present. Moonlight falling through the window on to a totally cleaned-up, unreally tidy kitchen. The pair of pheasants lie in the foreground, rotting slightly. The photo of the house, now on the mantelpiece. Moonlight falling across it. A slow cross-fade to:

38. INT. BATHROOM. NIGHT

JEAN *lying in the bath. She is stretched out, naked. There is a slight ripple as she reaches for the ashtray beside the bath, to knock the ash off the end of the cigarette. Then she takes a drag.*

39. INT. TRAIN. DAY

Flashback. The central aisle of a British Rail train careering fast through the countryside. It is full. Down the central aisle, a brown holdall on his back, comes MORGAN, *in a green anorak. He walks on down. He is looking for a seat. And yet he looks neither to one side nor the other.*

40. EXT. STATION. DAY

Flashback. A small country station, just two platforms on either side of the rails. The train rushes through at enormous speed. It is briefly shaken by the passage, then is still. The danger has passed.

41. INT. BOARDING HOUSE. DAY

Flashback. Coming up the darkened stairs of a small boarding house, a LANDLADY *is leading* MORGAN. *Then they come to a landing and she opens the door. The room is florally decorated, with wallpaper of roses and a quilt with creepers and flowers on it. He goes in. She stands outside.* MORGAN *looks at the cosy but desolate little room.*
LANDLADY: Do you know how long you'll be staying?
MORGAN: (*Closing the door*) Oh . . . just a couple of days.
    (*The* LANDLADY *goes.* MORGAN *lifts his holdall on to the bed.*

He unzips it. He takes out a pair of pyjamas which he puts on the bed. Then he sets a pile of books on the dressing table. He puts down a fat file, his thesis. We see the title: 'The Norman Village in the Thirteenth Century'. Then he reaches into the bottom of his holdall and takes out a gun. He goes to the window. It is covered by a thin pair of floral curtains. He draws one back. The window overlooks the town square in Wetherby. People are walking about, shopping, going about their work. They are predominantly middle-aged. MORGAN *looks down on them, the gun in his hand, the sniper thinking about possible targets. Some schoolchildren go by, an older woman.)*

42. EXT./INT. SQUARE. DAY

Flashback. From the square we look up to the first-floor window. MORGAN *standing at the window, the gun not visible, dark, to one side. The sniper in place.*

43. INT. JEAN'S HOUSE. DAY

The present. MARCIA *is sitting quite still by herself in the kitchen. Then* STANLEY *arrives with groceries in a brown paper bag and she gets up to greet him and take them from him.*

MARCIA: Ah, well done, Stanley. Thank you.
  (*She goes and puts them down on the kitchen slab.*)
  (*Calling upstairs*) Jean, we've got you some breakfast.
JEAN: (*Out of vision*) Thank you, Marcia. I'm just coming down.
  (MARCIA *nods at* STANLEY *who is holding the morning paper which he has picked up from the doormat.*)
MARCIA: Take the paper, Stanley, hide it. (*Calling upstairs again*) We brought you bacon and eggs.
  (*We glimpse the headline, 'Mystery Suicide at Wetherby Woman's House'.*)
STANLEY: Why hide it? After all, she was there when it happened.
MARCIA: Stanley, she doesn't want to be reminded. Would you?
  (JEAN *has appeared from upstairs. She is standing in the doorway. She is gaunt, sobered, changed.* MARCIA *turns from the stove.*)
  Good morning. No paper, I'm afraid. I think there's a strike.

(She turns to cook. STANLEY, *who is half-heartedly holding the paper behind his back, turns to* JEAN *with a look of 'What can you do?'* JEAN *goes to get a glass of water.)*

STANLEY: All right?

JEAN: Well, I'm not in the pink.

MARCIA: I shouldn't wonder.

STANLEY: Did you sleep?

JEAN: I had dreams.

*(*MARCIA *has begun to fry bacon.)*

MARCIA: Does anyone know why he did it? And why on earth did he choose to come and do it to you? It was me he met first. I don't know why I didn't *think* at the dinner. I'd already met him. He could have done it to me.

*(*JEAN *sits at the table, where the party was.)*

JEAN: I think the lonely recognize the lonely.

MARCIA: You're not lonely.

*(*JEAN *looks a moment to* STANLEY. MARCIA *shoves away the cat which has been attracted by the smell of bacon.* JEAN *looks away.)*

JEAN: I only want coffee.

MARCIA: Stanley, d'you mind? Go and do something useful. Do you know how to do it with a filter?

(She nods at the coffee grinder. STANLEY *goes to work it.* MARCIA *turns again from the frying pan.)*

Have you searched back? Over all your behaviour? You know, did you offend him in some way? That's what I've been thinking. Perhaps we upset him. Perhaps you looked like his mother, now that is possible. I read in a book . . .

*(*JEAN *interrupts, her voice clear and simple.)*

JEAN: I think it was more what we shared.

MARCIA: What's that?

JEAN: I told you. A feeling for solitude.

(There is a pause. MARCIA *is not convinced by this. She turns the bacon quite vigorously.)*

MARCIA: Well, you may have felt that. But to shoot your head off . . .

*(*JEAN *puts her hand to her mouth, interrupting her, this time urgently.)*

JEAN: Please, the bacon's too much.

MARCIA: Oh God, I'm sorry, it never occurred to me. I didn't think, oh Lord . . .

(*She turns, panicking, the pan in her hand, not knowing what to do with it.* STANLEY *goes to open the door.*)

STANLEY: Take it out.

MARCIA: Honestly, I'm sorry, Jean. It's out, it's almost gone . . .
  (STANLEY *stands at the door.* MARCIA *has gone. Through the window she is seen to be holding the frying pan under the garden hose which is attached to an outside tap.* STANLEY *and* JEAN *look at each other meanwhile. Then he speaks very quietly.*)

STANLEY: If you're frightened of loneliness, never get married.

JEAN: I'm not frightened. I'm hardened by now.

44. INT. THE MORTIMERS' HOUSE. DAY

Flashback, 1953. The YOUNG JEAN *is being led through the hall to the front room of the Mortimers' house. She is wearing a green floral dress and looks very fresh and clean.* JIM *is beckoning her in, to where his* MOTHER *is waiting in the front room. A small, eager woman of nearly fifty. There is a fire burning and tea is set out on the table.*

MRS MORTIMER: Come in, come in.
  (MR MORTIMER, *an equally small man in a suit, dressed for the occasion, gets up. The room could not be simpler. There is a fire burning in the grate.*)

MR MORTIMER: Ah.

MRS MORTIMER: Nice to meet you.

JIM: This is Jean.

YOUNG JEAN: Mrs Mortimer.
  (*They shake hands.*)

MRS MORTIMER: And this is Jim's father.

YOUNG JEAN: Hello.

MRS MORTIMER: Please sit down.

YOUNG JEAN: Gosh, look . . .

MRS MORTIMER: I baked you some scones. And there's Battenburg cake.
  (JEAN *smiles.*)

MR MORTIMER: You're looking very thin, lad.

JIM: Nay, I've been fine.

45. INT. THE MORTIMER' HOUSE. DAY

Later. They all have teacups and the remains of scones on their knees.

MR MORTIMER: And so you'd be giving up college?

YOUNG JEAN: No, I don't think so, Mr Mortimer.

MR MORTIMER: Ah.

YOUNG JEAN: Jim thought as he'd be away for so long and so often, it's better if I occupy myself. I think I have a place at the University of Hull.

MR MORTIMER: Are you sure?

(*He turns to* JIM, *who says nothing.*)

I don't think a woman who's going to get married should be thinking of going off away from her home.

YOUNG JEAN: But Jim won't be there. He'll be in Malaya.

MR MORTIMER: Ay, but he'd want to know that you're where you belong.

YOUNG JEAN: What difference can it make if he'd not be with me?

MR MORTIMER: He'll want to know you're at home.

(JEAN *looks a moment to* JIM *for confirmation to go ahead, for the conversation which has started out easily is becoming a little tense.*)

YOUNG JEAN: I can't see honestly it'll make any difference. Any home life we have is bound to be interrupted. At least from the start. We'll see each other so little for a bit.

MR MORTIMER: Seven years, is that right?

YOUNG JEAN: Well, not necessarily . . .

(*She is about to go on.*)

MR MORTIMER: Doesn't Jim speak?

(*There is a pause. They all look to* JIM, *who is quiet.*)

JIM: The Air Force'll give me a house later. When I'm back from active service. For now it's nice if Jean goes on with her books.

(*There is an awkward silence. To break it,* MRS MORTIMER *holds a plate out.*)

MRS MORTIMER: More Battenburg?

YOUNG JEAN: Did you bake it yourself?

MR MORTIMER: Don't be daft.

46. EXT. STREET. EVENING

Flashback, 1953. JIM *and* YOUNG JEAN *walking together along the deserted Oldham street. It is evening. There is nobody about and the light is about to go. Terraced redbrick houses on either side.*

JIM: You shouldn't worry.

YOUNG JEAN: They made me feel stupid.

JIM: Why?

YOUNG JEAN: Perhaps it is silly. Impractical. We've never really met, you and me. We're always so happy together. It never occurs to us that there's a world of people out there. We can't spend our life . . .

JIM: What?

YOUNG JEAN: Just . . . with the sheets up over our heads.
(*The whole street is now seen, bathed in exquisite light.*)

JIM: How could you make Battenburg? No one can *make* Battenburg. Half of it's pink.

YOUNG JEAN: Jim, I know. I was frightened. That's all.
(*They turn a corner. More streets, also deserted. A last bus.*)

JIM: Last bus.

YOUNG JEAN: Already?

JIM: You know nothing. This is a pig of a town.

47. INT. POLICE STATION. DAY

The present. A desk on which a row of photos has been laid out. Above, an Anglepoise lamp is the only source of light. The photos form a sequence: Morgan sitting at the table with his head blown off, in full-length shot, but each successive shot seeing him from a different angle. Then photos of the gun, and fingerprints. RANDALL, *the police doctor, showing them to* LANGDON.

RANDALL: The angle . . .

LANGDON: Yes.

RANDALL: . . . of the body means that murder is probably discounted. (*Points along the row to the close-ups of the gun.*) Forensic evidence, fingerprints. Nobody else has touched the gun. At the inquest I shall be arguing it's suicide.
(LANGDON *opens the curtains. We see outside his small, modern office to green fields stretching away.*)
You look disappointed.

LANGDON: No. Not at all.

48. EXT. JEAN'S HOUSE. NIGHT

LANGDON *stands in the garden looking up to the lit window of Jean's house. Then he moves away to his car.*

49. INT. POLICE STATION. DAY

Langdon's office now revealed in daylight. LANGDON *is adjusting a black tie which he is putting on in the mirror. The* POLICEWOMAN *is watching him.*

POLICEWOMAN: Where is it?

LANGDON: Derby. That's where he came from.

> (*A* POLICE SERGEANT, *uniformed, comes into his office, carrying a couple of chairs. He's followed by two other uniformed men, carrying more chairs.*)

SERGEANT: All right if we come in here, Mike? The lads need some space. New fire-hose demonstration.

LANGDON: Not in here, for Christ's sake.

SERGEANT: Not real hoses, you idiot. Slide show.

> (*They are setting chairs down around the desk where the photos of Morgan are still laid out.* LANGDON *looks across, unsure whether to object.*)

No problem. Mike? All right? Put your thumb up your bum for a bit?

> (LANGDON *turns and goes out of the room, into the main part of the police station, where a group of uniformed men are sitting laughing at a pornographic magazine. As he leaves, we just catch:*)
> (*To a uniformed man*) CID do fuck-all anyway.
> (*But* LANGDON *is already being called over to the group sitting on the edge of the desk.*)

FIRST POLICEMAN: Hey, Mike, look at this.

LANGDON: What is it?

> (*He goes over.*)

FIRST POLICEMAN: Famous people without their clothes on. Celebrity nudes.

SECOND POLICEMAN: Jesus, look at her.

LANGDON: What d'you mean?

> (*He frowns, not understanding. The* YOUNG POLICEWOMAN, *keeping her distance, looks disapprovingly.*)

SECOND POLICEMAN: Celebrity nudes! Here, look, here's Jackie
Kennedy . . .
POLICEWOMAN: All women.
FIRST POLICEMAN: Yup.
POLICEWOMAN: No men.
SECOND POLICEMAN: Is that meant to be Britt Ekland?
FIRST POLICEMAN: It's a very bad likeness. I think he must have
been in the bushes . . .
(*They laugh. The* POLICEWOMAN *stands alone.*)
POLICEWOMAN: Men would be taking the joke much too far.
(LANGDON *has picked up a large bunch of flowers, which is on
the counter. The* POLICEWOMAN *passes on her way out, her
anger still in her voice.*)
You don't need to take flowers.
LANGDON: I can't explain. I just thought I would.

50. INT. SCHOOL. DAY

JEAN *moves down the corridor to her classroom. An effort of will to
come in today. She listens to the familiar sounds of the teachers and
children, each in their classes. As she approaches her door,* ROGER
comes out, rather to her surprise. And he is surprised to see her.
ROGER: Oh, Jean . . . I'm sorry. I was settling your class. We
weren't expecting you.
JEAN: I decided I'd feel better if I came in.
ROGER: I gave them some books and told them to shut up.
JEAN: Good.
(*He looks at her, not knowing what to say.*)
ROGER: Well . . . you must come round to dinner.
JEAN: Yes, I'd like to.
ROGER: I mean, we must have you back. We don't see enough of
you.
(*He looks at her a moment, curiously. Then nods a little and
backs off down the corridor.*)
Bye.

51. INT. CLASSROOM. DAY

The class is quiet, all reading, as JEAN *comes in and puts her books
down on the desk. She forestalls all questions by her manner.*

95

JEAN: Right, come on, heads out of books, please everyone.
That's not how I teach – as you know.

GIRL: Mr Braithwaite said you weren't coming in.

JEAN: Well, then, you have a pleasant surprise. Board, please,
Marjorie.

GIRL: Please, Miss, I didn't hand in my exercise book.

(*A* GIRL *gets up to wipe the board.*)

JEAN: Shut up, sit down, open the window.

PUPIL: (*Calling from the back of the class*) You've still got a fag in
your mouth.

(JEAN *stops, smiles and takes it out. This little cabaret has put
everyone at their ease.*)

JEAN: Now. Good. Today we address the question: is
Shakespeare worth reading although it's only about kings?

52. INT. SCHOOL. DAY

The bell goes. The corridors are thronged with people. JEAN *comes
through the crowd as they go to the playground. Then she turns down a
corridor to where the locker room is. There in a darkened corner* SUZIE
BANNERMAN *is staring into the eyes of a fellow pupil, a* BOY *of
sixteen. They have been kissing.* JEAN *stops, unseen.* JEAN *looks a
moment. Then the* BOY *moves his hand on to* SUZIE's *skirt between her
legs.* JEAN, *unnoticed, turns to go back the way she came.*

53. EXT. JEAN'S HOUSE. DAY

Sitting outside the house in the sun on the doorstep is a GIRL *of
nineteen, in duffel coat and jeans. She is reading a paperback.* JEAN
*has returned from school with a lot of exercise books. And is standing
now at the garden gate. The* GIRL *looks up, aware of* JEAN's *gaze.*

KAREN: I'm sorry. I didn't mean to surprise you.

JEAN: It's all right.

KAREN: I should have rung.

(JEAN *can now see her clearly as she has got up. She is pale, very
slight and unassertive.*)

I've come from the funeral. I'm a friend of John Morgan's.

(*There is silence, as if* JEAN *is bracing herself for the next wave of
unhappiness. Then she moves towards the house.*)

JEAN: Come in.

54. INT. KITCHEN. DAY

KAREN *is sitting at the kitchen table, she is talking in a rather careless and withdrawn sort of way, without much purpose.* JEAN *is making tea, keeping busy, but attentive to everything* KAREN *says.*

KAREN: I had a kind of inkling he might do something silly. I always thought he was wierd.

JEAN: Were you at the same university?

KAREN: He was postgraduate. I'm just first year.

JEAN: Had you . . .

(JEAN *pauses. We are with her by the cooker.*)

. . . been going out with him?

KAREN: No. I never slept with him. We went to the cinema twice. We'd seen the film about the Indian.

JEAN: *Gandhi?*

KAREN: That's right. Afterwards he couldn't stop talking. He thought this, he thought that. The philosophy of non-violence and so on. And I really didn't think anything. Except obviously the film was very long. In that way we weren't even suited. I think he was trying to impress me.

(JEAN *smiles. She sets out fine china.*)

JEAN: He chose the wrong way.

KAREN: I like people who are just themselves. Not talking rubbish all the time.

(JEAN *looks at her, curious.*)

I know I shouldn't say that about anyone who's dead. But anyone who did what he did to you . . .

JEAN: It certainly upset me.

KAREN: Yes. I can tell.

(*There's a pause.*)

Then he started to pester me. I had to go to his professor to ask him to stop watching me. The worst was in the launderette.

(JEAN *is watching her, quite still.*)

I think it was me he wanted to do it to. And just by bad luck he did it to you.

(*The two women look at each other, suddenly close in their thoughts. But, as if fearing this closeness,* KAREN *turns away after a moment.* JEAN *has a teapot in her hand.*)

JEAN: Are you going back?

KAREN: When?

JEAN: This evening.

KAREN: Oh, I don't really have any plan. I only came over on an impulse. Then a policeman at the funeral gave me a lift.

JEAN: Who was that?

KAREN: He was called Langdon. I'd never have thought of it. It was his idea I should come.

55. INT. SPARE ROOM. DAY

The curtains are drawn in the spare room, which could not be barer. A bed unmade, no sheets. A simple table at the side. JEAN *is standing there as* KAREN *comes in. They stand a moment.*

KAREN: Yes, it's nice.

56. INT. JEAN'S HOUSE. DAY

KAREN *has a big plate of sausages and beans and toast in front of her. She is shovelling it in happily.* JEAN *is sitting opposite, watching. Like a mother and child.*

57. INT. JEAN'S HOUSE. NIGHT

Later. JEAN *is at the sink washing up.* KAREN *is sitting in an armchair at the other side of the room.*

JEAN: So how long did you know him?

KAREN: Who?

JEAN: John Morgan.

KAREN: Oh, him. I don't know.
    (JEAN *looks across.* KAREN's *mind is elsewhere.*)
    Do you have a television?

JEAN: Yes. I have one somewhere. Oh, I keep it under those books. (*Points to a pile of books and cardboard boxes in the corner.*) I hardly ever watch it.

KAREN: I watch it most evenings.

JEAN: Even at university? You watch it at university?

KAREN: They have a room you can sit in. (*Leaning over the back of the chair.*) Do you mind if I get it out?

58. INT. JEAN'S HOUSE. NIGHT

KAREN *sits watching a television comedy show. She is perfectly content.*

59. INT. JEAN'S HOUSE. NIGHT

Later. Now only the small light is on beside the armchair where JEAN *sits alone, reading. The door leading upstairs opens and* KAREN *comes in. She is wearing only a vest and pants and her hair is wet from the bath. Silently, she walks right past* JEAN *to the kitchen, collects a pair of nail scissors, and walks back past her.*
KAREN: I've finished in the bathroom. Good night.
    (*She goes out.*)

60. INT. LANGDON'S BATHROOM. NIGHT

MIKE LANGDON *stretched out in his bath. He has put the shaving light on, so he is barely lit. On the chair beside him, the black suit is folded with shirt and black tie. We think he is alone. But now a hand trails in the water by his knee. Crouched beside the bath on her knees is a blonde girl in her mid-twenties, pretty, slightly bland. There is a light behind her, so all we have is an impression of blond hair and warmth. We can tell she's just woken up.*
CHRISSIE: How was the funeral?
LANGDON: Ghastly. I had to go to Derby. And it started to rain.
    Only his mother left alive. She had no idea why he'd done it.
CHRISSIE: It seems as if neither do you.
    (*He smiles, acknowledging this.*)
LANGDON: Have you been riding?
CHRISSIE: Uh-huh. It's why I fell asleep. We broke in a new
    horse. So I'm saddle-sore.
    (*They both smile.*)
LANGDON: The problem is no crime has been committed. Killing
    yourself is legal. Even in front of somebody else.
CHRISSIE: Yes. Unless she did something to provoke him.
LANGDON: Yes.
    (*There's a silence.* CHRISSIE *gets up and goes out of the*
    bathroom, so LANGDON *has to call out:*)
    She'd only known him twenty-four hours.

(*No reply.*)
She is – what? – a teacher, a spinster, well loved, obviously
good at her job. Lives alone. Loved by her pupils. Did she
teach you?
(CHRISSIE *has reappeared with a large white towel which she
now holds out.*)

CHRISSIE: No, but I remember her. She was nice.
(LANGDON *does not move.*)

LANGDON: A good woman chosen for some reason as the victim of
the ultimate practical joke.

61. INT. JEAN'S HOUSE. NIGHT

Flashback. The beginning of the dinner party. ROGER *and* VERITY
are already seated in armchairs. MARCIA *leads into the room, her
present for* JEAN *under her arm. Then* JEAN *follows, beckoning*
MORGAN *into the room.* STANLEY *will be the last to arrive.*

VERITY: I don't watch that. I watch that thing on Sundays.

MARCIA: Hello, darling.

VERITY: Roger won't watch it because he says it's full of jokes
about blacks.

ROGER: Marcia. Hello. Stanley.
(ROGER *has stood up to kiss* MARCIA, *and shake hands with*
STANLEY. MARCIA *has already ducked down to kiss* VERITY,
who is not to be stopped in her train. JEAN *has gone straight to her
cooking, worried it is overheating, and we are with her now.*)

JEAN: Whoops, I need some more wine.
(*She heads back through the room.* STANLEY *holds out the bottle
he has brought.*)
No, red, it's for cooking.
(*She smiles at* MORGAN *as she goes out of the room to the corridor
for more. He smiles back, standing alone at the side of the room.*)

ROGER: I didn't say that, it's just that particular *kind* of joke
about blacks . . .

VERITY: I think if they want to be part of things, if they want to
be accepted as British, then they have put up with the fact
they will be a butt of people's humour. Just like mothers-in-
law.
(MORGAN *has gone over to look at* Jean's *books on the shelves,
by himself.* STANLEY *has taken his wine over to the kitchen.*)

STANLEY: (*Muttering,* sotto voce, *to* MARCIA) Do you know who that bloke is?

MARCIA: Stanley, don't be rude. He's a friend of Jean's.

(JEAN *has returned with wine, which she gives to* STANLEY *to open.*)

JEAN: Here you are. Will you open that for me? Roger, do you know John?

ROGER: (*Uncertainly*) Yea . . . gh.

JEAN: This is Verity.

(MORGAN *smiles.*)

VERITY: And if you actually *don't* make jokes about blacks it's a kind of reverse discrimination. It's a way of saying they don't really belong.

ROGER: No, you have to say . . .

VERITY: I don't *have* to say anything.

(MARCIA *has got a glass of white wine and is now moving to sit down and join in.*)

MARCIA: It's actually Jews who make jokes about Jews. When they do, for some reason, it's called Jewish humour . . .

ROGER: Marcia . . .

MARCIA: . . . but when we do it, it's called anti-Semitism. (*Smiles cheerfully at* MORGAN.) Don't you agree?

(JEAN *looks up from her cooking.* MORGAN *is watching her now from the far side of the room.*)

ROGER: You do realize this is an emotional argument?

VERITY: So?

MARCIA: (*Helping herself to hummus and pitta*) I'll be fined at Weight Watchers!

ROGER: It has no basis in logic at all.

VERITY: Oh, logic.

ROGER: Yes, you know, *logic,* that holds society together. *Logic,* that says people mustn't be allowed to go round killing each other . . .

STANLEY: Quite right.

ROGER: And that also tells you – please, I've started so please let me finish . . .

MARCIA: Magnus Magnusson!

ROGER: Logic also tells you that there must be constraints, and that if everyone went round saying what they truly feel, the result would be barbarism. (*Looks round the room. Quietly*)

And I prefer civilization. That's all.

(*There is a silence.* ROGER *smiles at* STANLEY *as if to say,
'There we are, that says it all.'* JEAN *is looking across at*
MORGAN *who has not lowered his stare throughout this
exchange. And now, in the silence,* JEAN *walks to him with a
glass of wine.* VERITY *starts again, low, much more bitter.*)

VERITY: Roger dislikes anyone being allowed to express
themselves. He sees it as a threat to property values.

ROGER: Darling, I don't think that's quite fair.

(JEAN *is staring at* MORGAN, *astonished by the evenness and
boldness of his look.*)

VERITY: He won't allow a firework display on the common for
fear a rocket lands on our thatched roof.

ROGER: Darling, now you're raising quite a different point.

VERITY: (*Suddenly shouting at him*) Life is *dangerous*. Don't you
realize? And sometimes there's nothing you can do.

(ROGER *is embarrassed. Everyone looks away.*)

ROGER: That's not true. I think you can always limit the danger.

STANLEY: (*Smiling*) What do you say, John Morgan? Speak up.
Intercede. It's a marriage. You must adjudicate between
warring parties.

(JEAN *looks across to see what* MORGAN *will say. His tone is as
level as ever.*)

MORGAN: Well, I can see both sides, I suppose.

62. INT. BEDROOM. NIGHT

The present. LANGDON *is sitting naked on the side of the bed.*
CHRISSIE, *in her dressing gown, is wrapped round his middle, curled
up. Only the bathroom light falls across the bed.*

LANGDON: If I said now, 'Go to Derek, divorce him . . .'

CHRISSIE: Oh, Mike . . .

LANGDON: Isn't it logical?

CHRISSIE: Aren't we happy . . .

LANGDON: Of course.

CHRISSIE: . . . as we are?

(*He takes her hand. She smiles.*)

Let's leave it. You spoil things if you push them too hard.

62. INT. BEDROOM. NIGHT

JEAN *lying awake in bed, her eyes wide open. After a silence she gets up and goes to the door, listening, silence.*

64. INT. LANDING. NIGHT

JEAN *stands in her nightdress on the landing. She pushes the door of the spare room open. Inside,* KAREN *is tucked up, fast asleep.* JEAN *looks at her from the door.*

65. INT. JEAN'S ROOM. NIGHT

Flashback 1953. At exactly the same angle as the previous shot, we see JIM *lying in a bed in the same place as Karen's. His eyes are closed.*

YOUNG JEAN: Jim. Jim, it's hopeless.

> (*We now see she is sitting on the radiator at the other side of the room, her books on the desk in front of her. She wears a dressing gown. She looks very thin and young.*)

JIM: What?

YOUNG JEAN: How can it work any more? Snatching time when my mum's out at cards, knowing we can't get married because of your parents.

JIM: We'll get married.

YOUNG JEAN: Eventually, yes. When you finally get back from Malaya. But it's so long. It makes everything seem pointless. Don't you think we should be sensible?

> (*There's a pause.* JIM *throws back the cover, crosses the room and kneels in front of her. He opens the two sides of her dressing gown lovingly. She is naked underneath. He looks into her eyes.*)

JIM: No.

66. INT. JEAN'S HOUSE. NIGHT

The present. KAREN *is sitting in the armchair doing nothing. In the front of the frame,* JEAN *is turning on a side lamp. She walks briskly across the room.*

JEAN: What do you think? Would you like to do something? Is there something you'd really like to do? I noticed there's a concert.

KAREN: No.
> (JEAN *has reached the other end of the room and turns.*)

JEAN: Karen, I feel there's a lot you'd like to tell me.

KAREN: Not specially.

JEAN: And sometimes you can't get it out.
> (*There is silence.* KAREN *says nothing.* JEAN *moves back, speaking very quietly, defeated.*)
> Yes. If you like I'll watch television with you.

67. EXT. STREET. NIGHT

Leeds. A darkened street. Rain. A woman is struggling along the street bent against the rain. It is JEAN. *In the darkness we can just make out the shape of the buildings – the old high arches and redbrick of the corn exchanges. A single lamp burns in an archway. Then she passes a huge piece of plate glass, with green and red light shining behind it, and steam running down it. The window of a large Chinese restaurant. She walks past, her head down. But then she turns back.*

68. INT. CHINESE RESTAURANT. NIGHT

Inside the restaurant is huge, with very bare tables at great distances. In the corner, some chefs are cooking in an open area with woks. JEAN *is sitting by herself, her face still wet, as if she has just dabbed it dry with a tissue, her wet coat behind her on the chair. At a large circular table some forty feet away from her, in the corner, a Chinese family are eating a cheerful meal. She watches them. They are very animated. She seems thoughtful. Then she looks up and* MIKE LANGDON *has come in with* CHRISSIE.

JEAN: Oh, well, goodness . . .

LANGDON: How are you? This is a coincidence. Do you know Chrissie? Jean Travers.

CHRISSIE: Hello.
> (*She is standing smiling beside him, and now reaches out her hand.* JEAN *smiles.*)

JEAN: (*Lightly*) Hello. Is this coincidence?

LANGDON: Good Lord, yes, I've given up thinking about you.
> (*There is a moment's pause. Then she gestures towards her table.*)

JEAN: Well, do please, yes. Or would I be interrupting?

LANGDON: Not in the slightest.

(*They sit down at her table.*)

Chrissie came into Leeds to pick up some gear.

CHRISSIE: I ride horses.

LANGDON: So I said I'd take her in, and we'll go to the cinema.
(*To the* WAITRESS, *who is handing him a menu*) Yes, thank
you.

CHRISSIE: Beer, please.

LANGDON: And me. And what are you doing?

JEAN: Oh, I don't know. (*Smiles at him.*) I've already ordered.

LANGDON: All right.
(*He nods at the* WAITRESS *who goes. There is a moment.* JEAN *is
looking at him as if deciding whether she can trust him. Then she
goes ahead.*)

JEAN: I'm afraid I got frightened.

LANGDON: Frightened?

JEAN: Yes.

CHRISSIE: Are you living on your own?

JEAN: No, I'm not, as it happens. A girl came to stay with me . . .

LANGDON: Oh, she stayed.

JEAN: Yes. (*To* CHRISSIE) A friend of John Morgan's. Have you
heard about this? So you know who I mean?
(CHRISSIE *nods.*)
Today I just . . . I was going to go home and then somehow I
couldn't face it. I just had to get out.

LANGDON: Why does Karen frighten you so much?
(*There's a silence.*)

JEAN: It sounds silly. I just can't get hold of her. She arrived on
my doorstep and I thought, oh, she really wants to talk to
me. Because she's had a similar experience, I suppose. But
it's as if she's missing a faculty. She seems to say something.
Then it just slips away. She has no curiosity. (*Shrugs slightly.*)
Then also . . . she asked to stay the night. I said, fine. Then
next day she didn't leave. Then yesterday she asked if she
could stay on.
(LANGDON *is looking straight at her.*)
It's a hard thing to say but I do see how Morgan became
obsessed with her.

LANGDON: Did he?

JEAN: Oh, yes. Violently, I think. She's the kind of girl people do
become obsessed with.

(*Suddenly* CHRISSIE *gets up.*)

CHRISSIE: Excuse me.

LANGDON: Why don't you just ask her to go?

JEAN: That's what I mean. She makes you feel that would be very rude.

69. INT. EXT. CAR. NIGHT

It is still raining. JEAN *is sitting in the front of* MIKE LANGDON's *car. She has wound her window down for fresh air.* CHRISSIE *is sitting at the back. The bleak industrial landscape of Leeds. As they draw up at the lights,* JEAN *turns and looks down the rows of abandoned terraced houses. In the middle of the road children have lit a bonfire, and are playing round it with sticks, and smashing bottles. There is a heavy silence between the three of them.*

70. INT. LANDING. NIGHT

KAREN's *face asleep in bed. Light falls across her face as* JEAN *and* LANGDON *open the door. They stand together on the landing, looking in.* JEAN *smiles, seeing the funny side of it.*

JEAN: Well, I mean, I can hardly wake her and say, 'This is my friend the policeman, and he offered to come round and tell you to leave.'

LANGDON: No.

(*She closes the door and edges past him. They are very close.*)

JEAN: I don't know. Everything gets to seem spooky.

(*She turns. It is dark. At the same moment they are aware that* MORGAN *was once here, alone with* JEAN. LANGDON's *eyes go up to the trap in the ceiling.*)

LANGDON: Is that where the tile was?

JEAN: Yes.

LANGDON: And he fixed it?

JEAN: What?

(*She frowns a moment.*)

LANGDON: How did he fix it? From the inside?

(*She does not answer. She moves past him and goes on down the stairs.*)

71. INT. KITCHEN. NIGHT

There is no light on in the kitchen, only moonlight, as JEAN *stands waiting for* LANGDON, *who appears a moment later. They look at each other across the kitchen.*

JEAN: Chrissie's waiting.

LANGDON: Yes.

(*There is a silence. Neither of them moves.*)

JEAN: Thank you for driving me home.

72. INT./EXT CAR. NIGHT

The little vanity light is on in the car, so CHRISSIE's *face is the only lit object in the night. A curious effect like an illuminated skull. She sits, waiting. Then the door of the farmhouse opens for* LANGDON *to come out. She looks across.*

73. INT. LIBRARY. NIGHT

Flashback. MARCIA *is sitting working at her desk in the British Library. It is an enormous open area, in which the only books go by on trolleys. The place is neon-lit and many people are at work, together.* MARCIA *becomes conscious of a man standing opposite her. It is* MORGAN, *in his anorak.*

MORGAN: I have a list of books I was hoping to borrow.

MARCIA: I'm sorry. You've been misinformed. This isn't a lending library, you know.

MORGAN: It's the British Library?

MARCIA: Oh, yes. But we don't lend books, or only under very special circumstances.

MORGAN: I have a letter from my professor.

(MARCIA *smiles, friendly.*)

MARCIA: I'm afraid that isn't going to be nearly special enough.

(*She returns to he work.* MORGAN *stands his ground.*)

MORGAN: Or just to look at the books, not borrow them . . .

MARCIA: Oh, yes, yes, yes, yes. You can *look* – if you are a registered user. You need authorization from the Librarian.

(*She smiles and returns to work. The encounter has already passed from her mind.*)

MORGAN: (*Blankly*) Yes, well I'll get that. Then I'll come back.

74. EXT. LIBRARY. DAY

Flashback. MORGAN *stands waiting outside the library. A modern white block, surrounded by barbed wire, in the middle of a field. There is a distorting mirror at the gate in which* MORGAN *watches a small group of women come down the road. He watches them go by.* MARCIA *is among them. He begins to follow.*

75. EXT. MARCIA'S HOUSE. NIGHT

Flashback. The lit windows of the top floor of Marcia's and Stanley's detached, leafy house. STANLEY *is in one room, changing into a pullover and old shirt, while* MARCIA *is moving from one room to the next, chatting all the time, dealing with her children.* MORGAN *stands watching in the bushes outside.*

76. EXT. MARCIA'S HOUSE. DAY

Flashback. Marcia's car is open outside her house. ROGER *is by it. We are watching* MARCIA *put a final cardboard box full of junk into its boot. She closes it and calls in through the front door:*

MARCIA: I'm off now, Stanley. Don't forget to unthaw their lunch.
> (*A child appears very briefly, whom* MARCIA *stoops down to kiss. A dog runs out.*)

77. INT. CAR. DAY

Flashback. The car now loaded. MARCIA *and* ROGER *side by side.*

MARCIA: It was funny. Clearing out all my stuff began to upset me.

ROGER: Really?

MARCIA: Don't you feel that?

ROGER: The past, you mean? (*Takes a shrewd look at her.*) That isn't like you.
> (*There is a silence between them.*)

MARCIA: Second-hand clothes . . .
> (ROGER *turns back.*)

ROGER: They say that murderers are drawn to the second-hand.

MARCIA: I hadn't heard that.

ROGER: Yes, there's a book . . .

MARCIA: You like murder, Roger.

ROGER: Yes, oh God, yes, I'm addicted. Yes, there's a theory that murder is characteristically committed by people who handle other people's things. In second-hand clothes shops, junk shops, markets.

(*He takes a quick look at her, but she is not reacting.*)

Self-improvement, that's another hallmark. People who teach themselves things, at home, at night, theories they only half understand. Informal education. A fantasy life of singular intensity.

MARCIA: Didn't you go to Switzerland last year?

ROGER: Oh, yes . . . I . . . yes, a package tour. To the Reichenbach Falls. There were forty of us from all over England. To see where Moriarty pushed Sherlock Holmes over. Wonderful countryside.

MARCIA: What did Verity think?

ROGER: Ah. She didn't come with me. No.

(*There's a pause.*)

A colleague from Home Economics came along.

(*There is a notable grimmer air to* MARCIA *as she swings the car round towards the church hall.* ROGER *tries to break the mood.*)

Do you like murder?

MARCIA: Not much. But I prefer it to romance.

78. INT. JUMBLE SALE. DAY

Flashback. MARCIA *is working at a stall in a busy jumble sale taking place in a church hall. Stalls with jams and cakes and toys.* MARCIA *working at the second-hand clothes stall. The other helpers are laughing with her at some clothes too bad even for the sale.* MORGAN *in his anorak is at the other end of the room, pretending to examine some toys, but sneaking looks at* MARCIA. MARCIA *is seen from* MORGAN's *point of view to be nodding vigorously, in agreement with a customer. Then she takes a pound note which she needs to get changed and crosses the room to the other side with it. The camera follows from* MORGAN's *point of view.*

There, at the other side, JEAN *is supervising a model desert into which you have to stick a pin to guess where the buried treasure is.* MORGAN *watches as* MARCIA *gets change from* JEAN, *but as* MARCIA

109

goes back to her stall, MORGAN's *stare stays on* JEAN, *who is now smiling and handing a pin to a little boy. She is quite oblivious of* MORGAN *at the other end. He looks content. He has found what he is looking for.*

79. INT. SCHOOL HALL. NIGHT

The present. JEAN *up a ladder adjusting a light for a small stage, which is at one end of the school hall. Four hundred seats have been set out, empty.* JEAN *has a cigarette in her mouth and her jeans on. She looks entirely in her element. She loves this work. The stage lights point at a medieval set. The light is hot, so she burns her hand, but she's used to it. In the back row,* KAREN *sits alone, four hundred empty seats in front of her.*

80. INT. SCHOOL. NIGHT

The school play. The hall now packed for the performance. The set on stage is black curtains with turrets and a landing place. Two boys in Renaissance costume – one with black headgear and statesman's robes, the other in the plain brown smock of a boatman. The lighting is full of colour – deep yellows and reds. The thickness and warmth of the atmosphere in the hall, plus the thickness of their make-up, gives the colours a lovely density.

'BOATMAN': The river flows dark tonight, Sir Thomas. Will you get on my boat?

'SIR THOMAS': Boatman, although I do not mean to deny you your livelihood I cannot take your boat. If I travel tonight, I will travel to the tower.

'BOATMAN': They say that is a place from which no man escapes.

'SIR THOMAS': Nay, not alive. But, boatman, we are set here on earth to do God's will, and if I do it tonight and in the fullness of my heart, he shall protect me, and lead me to a better place than any that we have known in this world.

'BOATMAN': Well, I wish you good fortune, sire.

'SIR THOMAS': I thank you. You are lucky to know no kings.
(*Takes out a gold sovereign.*) Here, take gold. (*Hands it over.*) Remember me in your prayers.
(*We go high above the hall as the curtains close and there is solid, warm and heartfelt applause.*)

81. INT. SCHOOL HALL. NIGHT

The chairs are all higgeldy-piggeldy, because parents and teachers are having a reception in the body of the hall. Parents and teachers stand in knots drinking wine or Coca-cola. Trays of food from cookery classes go round. Right by the stage KAREN *is being quizzed by a parent,* MR VARLEY, *who has gone up to her, seeing her standing alone.*

MR VARLEY: So who are you, my dear?

KAREN: Oh, I'm a friend of Miss Travers.

MR VARLEY: We all love Jean Travers. She's a wonderful character.

KAREN : Yes.

(*She smiles nervously and tries to look away.*)

MR VARLEY: So what do you do?

KAREN: Oh . . .

(*She shrugs and blushes.*)

MR VARLEY: What? Come on, answer. What's this? Too proud to talk to me?

(*She looks desperately across to where* JEAN *is seen to be in conversation with a couple of* PARENTS. *Their daughter is in Renaissance costume beside them.*)

Who are you? What do you do?

(*She moves away, but as she does, he reaches out and grabs her lightly by the arm.*)

Now look . . .

(*At the other side of the hall.* JEAN *in conversation with the* PARENTS.)

PARENTS: (*Alternately*) I won't want Janice to do A level English. Physics, that's the thing. We want her to get on. We bought her a home computer. We don't let her buy games. No *Star Wars*, nothing like that. ICI needs physicists, doesn't it?

(JEAN's *attention has gone to where* KAREN *has now dropped her drink on the floor, her face red.* MR VARLEY *is now trying to put a hand on her in a gesture of reassurance, but she is recoiling.*)

JEAN: Excuse me.

(JEAN *joins another* TEACHER *on her way to the incident. Another* PARENT *has joined in, trying physically to restrain* MR VARLEY.)

What on earth's going on?

TEACHER: It's one of the parents.

JEAN: How is it possible?

> (*Now there are raised voices.* KAREN *is about to cry. The* HELPFUL PARENT's *voice carries over the party.*)

HELPFUL PARENT: Leave her! Leave her alone!

KAREN: (*Shouts*) I wasn't saying anything. I didn't do anything!

> (MR VARLEY *blunders away through the party, bumping into people in a blind hurry to get out. The* TEACHER *shouts at his departing back:*)

TEACHER: Come back, Mr Varley – please.

> (JEAN *looks across at* KAREN.)

JEAN: Come on.

82. INT. SCHOOL CORRIDOR. NIGHT

JEAN *and* KAREN *come quickly down the corridor, which is not lit, towards Jean's classroom.* KAREN *has cut her hand on the glass.*

JEAN: What did he say?

KAREN: I don't know. What difference does it make? Why can't people leave me *alone*?

83. EXT. TOWER BLOCK. NIGHT

Flashback. The tower block at the University of Essex stands gaunt against the sky. More like a housing estate than a university. From one uncurtained window a light shines out. MORGAN *sitting at his desk, twelve floors up in the air.*

84. EXT. UNIVERSITY. NIGHT

Flashback. A gulch of tower blocks. They stand, lined up, sinister, desolated. Scraps of paper blow down between them. A scene more like urban desolation than a university. Concrete stanchions, deserted. A roadsign-like tin plate saying 'Keynes 2. Nightline' with an arrow.

85. EXT./INT. STUDENT CANTEEN. NIGHT

Flashback. Glass on both sides, so we can see right through – a few lonely students at the plastic tables.

86. INT. TOWER BLOCK. NIGHT

Flashback. An empty lift automatically opens its doors. Inside it is painted blue. Someone has scrawled, 'Fuck you All'.

87. INT. KAREN'S ROOM. NIGHT

Flashback. Karen's university room is very plainly furnished. A single light is on on the desk. There is a bed and a couple of posters, some books on the desk. We are behind KAREN *as she moves towards bed, taking off her top. She gets into bed in pants and vest. She turns her light off.*

88. INT. CLASSROOM. NIGHT

The present. JEAN *has not put the light on, so only the street light falls into the room, where* JEAN *is dabbing Dettol on to* KAREN's *hand with some cotton-wool she has got from the classroom medicine cupboard. When she speaks, it is very quietly.*

JEAN: What did he want?

KAREN: Who?

JEAN: That parent.

KAREN: Nothing. He just asked questions.

JEAN: What kind?

> (KAREN *is sulking, only just audible.*)

KAREN: Oh, you know, who was I? What was I doing here?

> (JEAN *looks at her, as if at last beginning to understand her.*)

JEAN: It sounds quite innocent.

KAREN: It's just that I hate it. All this asking that goes on. People digging about. The way people have to dig in each other. It's horrible.

> (JEAN *nods. She puts the kidney bowl aside. It is a little red from* KAREN's *blood.*)

JEAN: Did you say that to Morgan?

KAREN: Yes, well, I did.

JEAN: No wonder. I think you drove Morgan crazy.

> (KAREN *looks at her mistrustfully.*)

KAREN: I don't know what you mean.

JEAN: No, well, exactly. That's why.

> (KAREN *looks away.*)

Goodness, I'm not saying *deliberately*, I don't mean you
meant to . . .
KAREN: I don't do anything! I don't say anything!
(KAREN *looks for a moment fiercely at* JEAN.)

89. INT. CORRIDOR. NIGHT

Flashback. A screwdriver working at a lock. MORGAN *is on his knees
in the corridor outside Karen's room, unscrewing the entire lock. The
wood squeals slightly under the pressure. Then lock, handle, plate, all
come away in his hand. He looks a moment through the hole in the
door that is left. Then he pushes the door open.*

90. INT. KAREN'S ROOM. NIGHT

Flashback. We approach the bed. MORGAN *steps in front of us and
kneels down beside it.*
MORGAN: Karen. Karen. It's me.
(*An eye opens. Then, in panic, she wakes.*)
Karen, listen to me, please.
KAREN: Get out of here!
MORGAN: I only want to talk to you.
(*She gets up and runs along the bed. From the desk at the end she
starts picking up books and throwing them at him.*)
KAREN: Fuck you! Get out!
MORGAN: No, look, please, you must listen to me . . .
(*He grabs at her. They struggle and fall to the floor, her head
cracking as she goes down. Instinctively he lets go and she
scrambles out from under him, like an animal in panic. She starts
shouting.*)
I want some feeling! I want some contact! I want you fucking
near me!
(*She picks up the typewriter from the desk and throws it at him. It
slams into his chest with a terrible thud.*)
KAREN: Get out of here.

91. INT. CLASSROOM. NIGHT

The present. KAREN *passes* JEAN *on her way out of the classroom.*
JEAN *grabs at her wrist as she goes by.*

114

JEAN: Please don't go.

KAREN: You make an effort, you try to be nice, try to do anything
. . . you just get your head chopped off. Why *try*? (*Looks
angrily at* JEAN, *like a little girl*.) Anyway, tell me, go on, tell
me, since you're so clever, what did *you* do?

JEAN: Karen . . .

KAREN: If it wasn't an accident, I'd love to know what *you* did.
(*She turns and runs out of the room*.)

JEAN: Karen. Karen. Come back!

92. INT. CORRIDOR. NIGHT

The corridor deserted. KAREN *has run away and into the night.
Another corridor, also deserted. A third.*

93. INT. HALL. NIGHT

*The school hall, now empty and darkened. The chairs all over the
place.* JEAN *comes in, stands a moment. But there is no one there.*

94. INT. MARCIA'S ROOM. NIGHT

Flashback, 1953. YOUNG MARCIA *is sitting on the bed in her dressing
gown in a room much more feminine in its decoration than Young
Jean's. Very fifties. The effect is made odd by the bottles of light ale
they are both holding.* YOUNG JEAN *is on the other side of the room in
her coat.*

YOUNG JEAN: (*Quietly*) If I had the guts I'd just say to him,
'Look, I don't want you to go, I need you.'

YOUNG MARCIA: Why don't you say that?

YOUNG JEAN: Because to him, it's everything. Being an airman is
everything. Until he gets to Malaya he isn't going to feel
being an airman is real.

YOUNG MARCIA: And what do you feel?

YOUNG JEAN: I don't know. Of course, I don't like it . . .

YOUNG MARCIA: Are you frightened he's going to get killed?
(JEAN *looks at her in astonishment.*)

YOUNG JEAN: No. No, of course not. I hadn't even thought of it.
Why do you say that?

YOUNG MARCIA: I'm sorry. I didn't think.

(*There's a pause.*)

YOUNG JEAN: If you want the truth it's this: with him I can't talk. With him I can't say anything I feel. Because . . . because I read books I feel for some reason I'm not allowed to talk. For that reason, there is always a gulf. (*Crosses the room and puts her empty bottle down.*) It doesn't seem a very good basis for marriage.

YOUNG MARCIA: No. I suppose.

(JEAN *goes and embraces* MARCIA, *in fondness.* MARCIA *smiles too.*)

(*Tentatively*) Perhaps . . . perhaps sex isn't everything.

YOUNG JEAN: No.

(JEAN *grins widely. They both burst out laughing at the unlikeliness of this statement.*)

YOUNG MARCIA: It's time that you talked to him.

YOUNG JEAN: Soon he'll be gone.

95. INT. LANGDON'S HOUSE. DAY

CHRISSIE *is standing in the bathroom, looking in the mirror. She stands a moment, then smiles, as if in affection for everything around her. Then she turns and goes into the bedroom. A suitcase, already nearly full, is open on the bed. She looks at it a moment. The phone beside the bed begins to ring. She pauses a moment, then goes to the chest of drawers to get more stuff to put in the suitcase.*

96. EXT. LANGDON'S HOUSE. DAY

Outside a man is waiting in a Land-Rover. As he watches her close the door, he gets out of the car. He is about fifty, bald, countrified, in green Huskie jacket and wellingtons. CHRISSIE *comes down the path.*

97. INT. LANGDON'S OFFICE. DAY

LANGDON *is sitting in his office at the police station. He has the phone to his ear. It is ringing out. He looks up and the* POLICEWOMAN *who was at the house on the day of the suicide is standing there.*

POLICEWOMAN: There's a man out here to see you.

(LANGDON *nods and puts down the phone. He goes out into the main office and goes to the desk. On the other side, a man is*

sitting, his coat wrapped over his knee. It is ROGER
BRAITHWAITE. *He looks up.*)

98. INT. JEAN'S HOUSE. NIGHT

JEAN *sitting by herself in the dark watching television. It is a discussion
programme.*

CHAIRMAN: (*On the screen*) And so what would you say we mean by
    lying?

BEARDED MAN: (*On the screen*) Well, it's not telling the truth. At
    its most basic. Or at least not telling what we believe to be the
    truth. That's lying. But there's also a kind of lying by
    omission, failing to say something which is clear to us, leaving
    something unsaid, which we know we ought to say. Which is
    in a way morally an equal crime.
    (*There is a knock at the door.* JEAN *turns, slightly dazed. She
    touches the switch of her remote-control unit.*)

CHAIRMAN: (*On the screen*) But do you think . . .
    (*He goes to silence.* JEAN *turns on a lamp. She opens the door,*
    LANGDON *is standing there.*)

LANGDON: Hello. How are you?
    (*She looks at him a moment.*)

JEAN: You look pretty shattered.

LANGDON: Yes.
    (*She lets him in, then goes to the television to turn it off. Pictures of
    Nixon at his most triumphant, arms over head, briefly seen before
    she kills it.*)
    I'm afraid I've had trouble at home. Chrissie went back to her
    husband.

JEAN: She had one already?

LANGDON: Oh, yes. Who she told me she never saw any more. But
    all the time – I don't know – it turns out I was a sub-plot. The
    real story was happening elsewhere.

JEAN: That's a terrible feeling.

LONGDON: The worst.
    (*There's a slight pause.*)
    It's shaken my whole idea of myself. What I'm doing as a
    policeman. If the day was no good, if it was awful or silly, I could
    always go back to Chrissie and laugh. But now it turns out, she
    wasn't really with me. She laughed. But she was elsewhere.

JEAN: What's he like?

LANGDON: Awful. He's the sort of man who keeps sheep. I mean, for God's sake, if you want wool, go and buy it in a shop.

(JEAN *stands a moment, not knowing what to say*.)

Listen . . . I'll tell you why I'm here. I was piecing together the evening . . .

JEAN: Oh God, can't you leave it?

(LANGDON *is surprised by her sudden rudeness*.)

LANGDON: Well, yes. This is just an amateur's interest.

JEAN: All right.

(*She nods, allowing him to go on*.)

LANGDON: It's just . . . there was food and then there was talking. Then you went upstairs. Didn't you have a few moments alone with him? You were together. What did you talk about?

JEAN: Fixing the roof.

(*There is a pause*.)

LANGDON: It's just Roger . . . your colleague . . . Roger says when you came back he remembers you'd changed.

JEAN: Changed?

LANGDON: Not, I don't mean, I'm not saying as a person. Your clothes.

JEAN: I put on trousers. I'd snagged my stocking. (*Moves away. Cheerfully*) Would you like some tea? Gosh, poor you, so how are you managing alone?

(*But his gaze is steady*.)

LANGDON: Don't you think you should tell me?

JEAN: What?

LANGDON: What happened? Was it your fault?

(*She looks at him nervously, trapped at last. Then she goes and sits on the sofa. Her shoulders sag, as if the whole effort of the last weeks were over*.)

JEAN: I think, in a way, it's because he was a stranger. I'm not sure I can explain. Because I didn't know him, now I feel him dragging me down. I thought I could get over it. But everywhere now . . . the darkness beckons. (*Looks across at him*.) These things become real. He wants me down there.

LANGDON: Well, you have to fight.

JEAN: I've fought. How dare you? (*Suddenly becomes angry, beginning to shake*) I've fought for three weeks. And you didn't help. Sending me that miserable little girl. What gives you that right? To meddle?

(*He doesn't answer.*)

The police who always bring sadness.

(LANGDON's *gaze does not falter.*)

LANGDON: I'm going to sit here. I won't go away.

99. INT. STORE. DAY

Flashback. At once the bell of the shop ringing as JEAN *comes into the small grocery store.* MR KARANJ *stands behind the delicatessen counter.* JEAN *goes round, tumbling things into a wire basket.*

MR KARANJ: Ah, you are holding a dinner, Miss Travers.

JEAN: Who told you?

MR KARANJ: The whole town has heard.

    (MR KARANJ *smiles*)

JEAN: No, just some friends round to supper.

MR KARANJ: Yes. Mrs Pilborough was in.

    (JEAN *passes a man whose face we do not see. He is wearing an anorak.*)

She is taking wine to your dinner. A bottle of Muscadet. She asked if I knew what you were cooking.

JEAN: Chicken.

MR KARANJ: Perfect. I felt she was safe.

    (MR KARANJ's *daughter,* SHARMI, *has appeared at the bottom of the stairs which lead to their flat above the shop. She stands, framed in the doorway, as* JEAN *dumps her goods on the counter.*)

JEAN: If I remember anything else, will you send Sharmi round?

MR KARANJ: She cannot leave the shop after dark. She has never been out in the evening. Have you, Sharmi?

    (SHARMI *smiles ambiguously.*)

It is a matter of pride to me. She has never once left her home in the dark. (*Turns and addresses her sharply.*) Khari kyoa ho. Jao oopar jao.

SHARMI: Jati hoon papaji. Aap ki chai tayar hai. Aap jalli peelo.

    (*She turns and looks at* JEAN, *smiling a second, then she disappears into the dark upstairs. We travel sideways and see the man whose face we missed. It is* MORGAN. *He is watching.*)

JEAN: (*Out of vision*) Thank you. That's all.

100. INT. JEAN'S HOUSE. DAY

Flashback. JEAN *puts her shopping down on the work surface, then turns to the cookbook. It is propped up already. She flips it open. It says 'Coq au vin'.*

101. EXT. JEAN'S HOUSE. EVENING

Flashback. MARCIA *coming up the path to the house with* STANLEY *following. It is evening and the lights are on in the house.* MARCIA *talking as she comes.*

MARCIA: Now, Stanley, don't drink too much, please. Last night you were stupid with gin.

STANLEY: I like gin.

(*As if from the bushes, unremarked,* MORGAN *steps into frame, suddenly beside them, already waiting.*)

MARCIA: Ah.

MORGAN: I rang the bell.

MARCIA: There's no need. She can see us anyway.

(MARCIA, *puzzled for only a second, now taps on the window, and waves vigorously.* JEAN, *her back turned to her cooking, now looks to the window.*)

Hello, Jean!

(MORGAN *is smiling at* STANLEY.)

MORGAN: I'm John Morgan.

(JEAN *opens the door welcomingly.*)

JEAN: Ah, hello, hello, you brought an extra.

STANLEY: (*Frowns.*) No.

JEAN: Come in, come in, come on, the more the merrier.

(MORGAN *holds out his hand to* JEAN, *as* MARCIA *sweeps on into the house.* STANLEY *is left with the bottle of wine he has brought.*)

MORGAN: John Morgan.

MARCIA: I've already told Stanley he's not to get drunk.

(*Everyone has moved on into the house, except* STANLEY, *who alone has noticed something odd.*)

STANLEY: What?

102. EXT. AIRFIELD. NIGHT

Flashback, 1953. By one of the dormitory sheds YOUNG JEAN *stands alone. Suddenly a shaft of light falls on the wet pathway and* JIM *steps out, fully dressed in his RAF uniform, carrying his rolled-up luggage, his buckles gleaming, the perfect figure of the airman.*

JIM: Well, what d'you think?

YOUNG JEAN: Well, of course, you look wonderful.
> (*There is a moment's pause. They are some way apart.*)

JIM: You don't like me going.

YOUNG JEAN: What makes you say that? I've never said that. I've encouraged you. I can see it's your happiness. You've never been happier than today. I've always told you, you must do what you want.

JIM: Yes. You've supported me. And I've been grateful. I'll come back. We'll have a house.
> (*There is a pause.*)
> If you want to stop me, you can.
> (*She shakes her head.*)

YOUNG JEAN: No, I'll study. I've lots to do.

JIM: Are you being true with me?

YOUNG JEAN: True? What does it mean?
> (JIM *waits, serious.*)

JIM: If you've anything to say, speak it now.
> (*There are tears in her eyes. She shakes her head.*)

YOUNG JEAN: Nothing.
> (*He moves towards her and kisses her.*)

JIM: Goodbye.
> (*They begin to walk. We are above them. It is apparently deserted till we turn the corner. All over the rest of the airfield,* AIRMEN *are making their way with bags over their shoulders. Four great planes are waiting. Commanding officers with lists of where they're to go. Wives standing waving at the side of the field. The men thicken into a crowd, going in one direction, till* JEAN *is the only woman among them.* JIM *turns, and goes, joining the flow.* JEAN *stands alone as the other men sweep past her. One of the great planes shudders into life, with a roar.* JIM *turns at the steps, and mouths the word 'Adios'. He goes in.* JEAN *stands alone on the pathway, her dress blowing from the propellers. The plane moves towards us.*)

103. INT. JEAN'S HOUSE. NIGHT

Flashback. The dinner party at its most raucous and warmest. A pitch of happy declamation. STANLEY *is suddenly the most vociferous of all.*

STANLEY: Revenge! That's what it is. Revenge! That's what she's doing.

VERITY: Who?

STANLEY: The Prime Minister. Taking some terrible revenge. For something. Some deep damage. Something inside. God knows what. For crimes behind the privet hedge. And now the whole country is suffering. And yet we've done nothing to her.

ROGER: Do you think that?

JEAN: (*Setting the dish down*) Coq au vin.
(*She takes the lid off. It looks fantastic.*)

ROGER: Ah, marvellous.

MARCIA: Stanley, you're drunk.
(JEAN *dishes it out with green salad and French bread.*)

STANLEY: Drunk? Yes. Drunk and disorderly. Where once I was orderly. My thoughts were once in neat rows. Like vegetables. Pegged out, under cloches. I kept my thoughts under cloches. But now they grow wild. (*Turns to* MORGAN.) You wouldn't know, I'm the local solicitor, the town's official sanctifier of greed. Those little unseemly transactions. I see people as they truly are.

MARCIA: Nonsense.

STANLEY: I remember once my father, also a solicitor, said to me, 'I have learnt never to judge any man by his behaviour with money or the opposite sex.' Yet it is my own saddened experience, that those are the *only* ways to judge them.

VERITY: Salad?

STANLEY: Thanks.
(*The hot chicken is variously admired.*)

MARCIA: Stanley thinks good of nobody . . .

STANLEY: Not true. I *expect* good of nobody. And am sometimes pleasantly surprised. And when I find good . . . my first feeling is one of nostalgia. For something we've lost. Ask John Morgan.
(*He turns to* MORGAN. *There's a pause.*)

MORGAN: Well, I don't know. I only know goodness and anger and revenge and evil and desire . . . these seem to me far better words than neurosis and psychology and paranoia. These old words . . . these good old words have a sort of conviction which all this modern apparatus of language now lacks.

(*People have stopped eating and are looking at him. There is a silence.*)

MARCIA: Ah, well, yes . . .

MORGAN: We bury these words, these simple feelings, we bury them deep. And all the building over that constitutes this century will not wish these feelings away.

(*These is a pause.* JEAN *looks at him. He looks steadily back.*)

ROGER: Well, I mean, you'd have to say what you really mean by that.

MORGAN: Would I?

ROGER: Define your terms.

(MORGAN *looks at him.*)

MORGAN: They don't need defining. If you can't feel them you might as well be dead.

104. EXT. CLOUDS. NIGHT

Flashback, 1953. Totally silent. Model shot. Jim's big troopcarrier flies through the night. No noise. The dark shape moving through the clouds.

105. EXT. AIRFIELD. NIGHT

Flashback, 1953. Silent also. We crane down from way above the field as YOUNG JEAN *walks back, alone. The field now deserted.*

106. INT. JEAN'S HOUSE. NIGHT

Flashback. The dinner party. MORGAN *looks up to the ceiling.*

MORGAN: It looks as if your roof is in trouble. I'm very practical.

(JEAN *looks a moment round the company.*)

JEAN: Right.

107. EXT. STREET. NIGHT

Flashback, 1953. JIM *in a street in Singapore, which is the poor area, just huts and squatters and roadside lights. He is being as patient as he can with the attentions of his cockney friend,* ARTHUR, *who pursues him.*

JIM: No, get away, I don't want to.

ARTHUR: Is it your girl? Is that what it is?

(ARTHUR *takes* JIM *by the arm and stops him walking on.*)

Jim, you're a crazy man. You've got to go to the brothel. You're here for six months, you can't just give up.

JIM: Well, that's what I'll do.

(*He tries to move off, but* ARTHUR *takes his arm again.*)

ARTHUR: There's a good place – listen – off limits. Not a brothel.

JIM: I don't want to go.

ARTHUR: Please, it's . . . it'll be like the local. Only better.

(*He has taken him by the shoulder and now looks him in the eye.*)

Jim. Jim, take me seriously. I can give you a very good time.

(JIM *smiles.* ARTHUR's *humour has won him.*)

JIM: All right. But no fucking.

ARTHUR: I can give you a no fucking good time.

108. EXT. SHACK. NIGHT

Flashback, 1953. A piece of wasteground. On it a single shack, a simple wooden building, with light shaded at its windows. JIM *and* ARTHUR *appears in the foreground.*

ARTHUR: Show me your money.

(JIM *has a roll of notes which he takes from his pocket.* ARTHUR *peels half off and hands it back to him.*)

Put that in your shoe.

(*They both stoop down. They put notes in their shoes. Then stand.*)

Let's go in.

109. INT. JEAN'S HOUSE. NIGHT

Flashback. JEAN *goes up the stairs, leading. It is very dark.* MORGAN *is following behind.* JEAN *stops dead, without looking round.*

JEAN: What you said . . . what you said about those feelings. It did make such sense.

MORGAN: Yes, I thought you'd understand me.
> (*He waits a moment. She points to the ladder and trap that lead to the roof.*)

JEAN: It's here.
> (MORGAN *moves past her, very close indeed. He goes up the ladder and lifts the trap.* JEAN's *point of view of him from below.*)

110. INT. SHACK. NIGHT

Flashback, 1953. A group of Malays are sitting in a circle, on boxes, in a plain wooden room as ARTHUR *and* JIM *push open the wooden door. There is no sign of the room having any function but the game. It stops. A* YOUNG MALAY *who is lounging against the wall moves towards them.* ARTHUR *speaks, exaggeratedly, English to the foreigner.*

ARTHUR: Take part in your game. We would like to. We have heard. The best game of poker in Malaya.
> (*The* YOUNG MALAY *looks to the group. A fatter, older Malay nods.*)

YOUNG MALAY: OK.
> (*There is silence as* ARTHUR *and* JIM *sit on boxes to join the game. The cards are dealt. Then an opium pipe is passed to* ARTHUR. JIM *tries to warn him, but* ARTHUR *cuts him off.* ARTHUR *accepts unhesitatingly. He begins to smoke. A gesture of brio.*)

ARTHUR: Thanks very much.

111. INT. LANDING. NIGHT

Flashback. MORGAN *comes down the ladder with the torch.* JEAN *waits on the landing. The scene exactly as we saw it earlier.*

JEAN: A slate fell in the night. I was frightened to go up there.

MORGAN: It's all right.
> (*He is quite still on the ladder.*)
> Shall we go down?
> (*He begins to move*).

112. INT. SHACK. NIGHT

Flashback, 1953. At once ARTHUR *slumps to the floor, passing out from the opium.* JIM *gets up in panic, his crate falling behind him. The* YOUNG MALAY *intercedes.*

YOUNG MALAY: It's OK. It's OK.

JIM: What have you given him?
> (*The two men on either side of* ARTHUR *take hold of his body and start to drag it across the room.*)

YOUNG MALAY: I have something. . . Hold him!

JIM: *DON'T DRAG HIM!*
> (*At once* JIM *is restrained as he tries to move across. The* FAT MALAY *nods at the other* MEN. ARTHUR *is deathly white.*)
> Who runs this game! I thought you were the boss.
> (*He looks at the* FAT MALAY, *who turns away.*)

YOUNG MALAY: No fighting, please!
> (ARTHUR's *body is pulled at alarming speed behind bead curtains. The* YOUNG MALAY *is now opposite* JIM.)
> I have something. Step in here. I will give you some medicine for him.
> (*He gestures to the bead curtains.* ARTHUR *has vanished behind them.* JIM's *face.*)

113. INT. LANDING. NIGHT

Flashback. MORGAN *has reached the bottom of the ladder.* JEAN, *standing still, suddenly and impetuously grabs at him with her hand as he is about to move by. It is as if the gesture is suddenly irresistible, and he turns and embraces her in return. They begin frantically clutching at each other's clothes. The feeling is violent, hysterical. He pulls her down towards the floor.*

114. INT. SHACK. NIGHT

Flashback, 1953. JIM, *sweating, looks to the room and begins very slowly to walk towards it.*

115. INT. LANDING. NIGHT

Flashback. As JEAN *and* MORGAN *go down on the floor, her legs slip along the board, catching a nail in the skirting board. Her stocking rips. At once a thin line of blood.*

116. INT. SHACK. NIGHT

Flashback, 1953. JIM *parts the bead curtain. The* YOUNG MALAY *stands opposite him and smiles.*
YOUNG MALAY: English airman.
> (*Subliminally, for a moment,* JIM *turns to see* ARTHUR's *body lying on the ground, before he is taken from behind by the* YOUNG MALAY *who wraps his arm round his throat.*)

117. INT. JEAN'S HOUSE. DAY

Flashback. JEAN *at the sink. We have* MORGAN's *point of view. We do not see him. Instead we travel slowly towards* JEAN *in a movement that approaches her back.*
JEAN: I love the slow evenings once the summer begins to come. It doesn't get dark until eight.
> (*We move right in on her.*)

118. INT. SHACK. NIGHT

Flashback, 1953. The YOUNG MALAY *passes a knife across* JIM's *throat. Blood pours from the wound.*

119. INT. JEAN'S HOUSE. DAY

Flashback. JEAN *looking in amazement at* MORGAN *who is now sitting at the table.*
JEAN: Absurd! It's impossible!
MORGAN: No.
> (MORGAN *lifts the revolver and blows his brain out.*)

120. INT. SHACK. NIGHT

Flashback, 1953. Repeated action, shown three times: the knife goes back to the beginning of the action each time across JIM's *throat. Each time blood spurts in a red line across the neck.*

121. DREAM

Process shot: the YOUNG JEAN, *naked, runs down a corridor at full pelt. The walls are on either side of her but as she runs they recede. Her figure stays the same size in proportion to the walls, which go endlessly by. She strains, to no effect.*

122. INT. JEAN'S HOUSE. DAY

Flashback. JEAN *standing at the sink.* MORGAN *sitting at the kitchen table, slumped across, his head blown off.*

123. INT. LANDING. NIGHT

Flashback. MORGAN *is on top of* JEAN, *as if about to make love to her. It is very quiet suddenly. Their faces are very close together. We are way above them, and as they speak we come closer slowly, creeping in. We can only just hear.*

MORGAN: Listen, I know you're in trouble.

JEAN: What?

MORGAN: You're in trouble. Like me.

JEAN: I don't know what you mean.

MORGAN: Come on.

JEAN: No.

MORGAN: You're lonely.

JEAN: Yes, well, I'm lonely, I'm not in trouble.

MORGAN: Please don't argue with me. All that hope coming out of you. All that cheerful resolution. All that wonderful enlightenment. For what? For nothing. You know it's for nothing. Don't tell me that cheerfulness is real.

JEAN: Yes, of course.

MORGAN: You and I – we understand each other.

JEAN: What? No . . . what?

MORGAN: You fake. You fake all that cheerfulness.

JEAN: No, please. It's who I am.

MORGAN: Then why did you lead me up here?

JEAN: I didn't.

MORGAN: Liar! (*He twists her head and speaks into her ear.*) You know. You know where you're looking.

JEAN: I don't.

MORGAN: You've been here. Where I am.
>   (*She begins to struggle free of him, panicking, realizing the extent of his madness. At once he grabs at her sweater, but she wrenches herself free.*)
JEAN: I haven't. I'm sorry. I haven't been where you are. I have to change.
>   (*She has struggled up. There is blood running down her stocking.*)
MORGAN: No.
JEAN: Yes. *Please.*
>   (*She is about to move towards her room, when he grabs her arm. He looks at her with a sudden, terrifying ferocity.*)
MORGAN: *You will.*

124. EXT. JEAN'S HOUSE. NIGHT

Flashback. The house seen from a great distance. Lit windows in the night. The front door opens. The end of a dinner party. The sound of STANLEY, *very distant.*
STANLEY: Out into the night, and then goodnight again! Whoops!
>   (*He falls, not badly, but enough to see him to the ground.* JEAN *is out there in front of him.*)
MARCIA: Oh, Stanley . . .
STANLEY: (*Getting up*) The drinking of whisky . . . the drinking of gin . . .
>   (*He smiles.* JEAN *has gone to the garden gate to see everyone away, and now turns.* MORGAN *has appeared in the doorway, seen through the shapes of the tottering* STANLEY *and the others.*)
MORGAN: It's been very pleasant. Would you mind if I came round again?
>   (*They look at each other, across the distance.* STANLEY *suddenly addresses the night.*)
STANLEY: God, look at it! The night! The stars! Our lives!
>   (MORGAN *suddenly smiles.*)

125. INT. JEAN'S HOUSE. NIGHT

The present. Night has come as JEAN *and* LANGDON *have sat together, the story unfolding. Now* LANGDON *gets up and, without looking at* JEAN, *he turns thoughtfully and walks to the far side of the*

*room. There he turns, and then looking at her, walks quickly back
across the room and takes her in his arms.*

LANGDON: There. There. Hold me tight.

> (*They embrace. Then he begins to kiss her, softly, kindly, all over
> her face. She kisses him. They rub their faces together, all the
> tension going out of them. They kiss again, their faces going down
> together side by side. All the memories go, as they embrace, their
> hands all over each other. Fade.*)

126. EXT. JEAN'S HOUSE. DAY

Next morning fades up. The house looks gentle, English, benevolent.

127. INT. SCHOOL CORRIDOR. DAY

JEAN *walks along the busy corridor, saying 'Good morning' distantly
to various pupils as she passes.* ROGER *comes down the corridor. He
looks down. She takes no notice. They pass. She goes on into the
classroom.*

128. INT. CLASSROOM. DAY

JEAN *comes into her class. It is cheerful and noisy. It quietens down on
her appearance.*

JEAN: Right everyone, good morning. First day of the week.
Monday morning. Welcome. Windows, please. Gosh, a dirty
blackboard already. (*Gets out a big book.*) Register. (*Looks
round the class.*) Please, where's Suzie?
(*There's silence.*)
Does anyone know?

JOHN: (*The sly boy*) She's run away to London.

GIRL: With Alfred Egerton. In Science Fifth.
(*The* GIRL *giggles. Another* GIRL *thinks this the most hilarious
thing.*)

JEAN: Has she been in touch with her parents?

GIRL: Oh yes, miss.

JEAN: Good.

BOY: (*From the back of the class*) She said she couldn't see the
point of school.

JEAN: (*Serious, quiet*) No, well, sometimes I have that problem.

(*Looks round the class.*) Anyone else? Anyone else want to go?
(*There is a silence, profound, as if recognizing her seriousness.*)
You are free. You are free to go if you wish.
(*The whole class seen in wide shot, quite still. Then* JEAN *speaks very quietly.*)
Right then, for those of us still remaining – us maniacs, assorted oddballs, eccentrics, folk who still feel that school is worthwhile, I suggest we keep trying. All right, everyone?
(*She looks round smiling. They are pleased by this speech.*)
Good. Then let's work.

129. INT. LANGDON'S HOUSE. DAY

Langdon's room. LANGDON *is standing on one side of the room in his shirtsleeves, tie and suit trousers. His jacket lies across the unmade bed on the other side of the room. He is looking across at it. Then he moves across the room. His wallet and keys are lying on the dressing table. He opens the wallet. Inside, his CID card. He takes it out, looks at it, then tears it up into little pieces. They sprinkle down on the floor.*

130. EXT. LANGDON'S HOUSE. DAY

We go high above the housing estate as MIKE LANGDON *comes out of his front door in pullover and trousers and walks off down the road. A hundred little brick houses stretch away into the distance. The empty tarmac road glitters.*

131. INT. PUB. DAY

JEAN *sits alone in the pub. A wide shot, sitting alone in the smoke. Then, after a while,* STANLEY *appears.*
JEAN: How are you?
STANLEY: How are you?
    (JEAN *smiles.*)
JEAN: I'm better. How's Marcia?
STANLEY: Oh, she's tremendous. Yes. The Charity Bridge
    Tournament takes all her time.
    (*The* BAR GIRL *comes with a bottle of white wine. She puts it down. She is very young.* STANLEY *stares up at her, dazzled by her beauty. Then they watch her go, saying nothing.*)

When you're a boy, you think, oh, it's so easy. Always wipe
the slate and move on. Then you find, with the years, you
become the prisoner of dreams.

(JEAN *nods slightly*.)

JEAN: A girl ran away this morning.

STANLEY: Good luck to her.

JEAN: Yes. Good luck.

(STANLEY *lifts his glass*.)

STANLEY: To all our escapes.

(*They drink. We pull back. They are two among many. The low
sound of conversation in the pub. They look around them. Fade.*)

DREAMS OF LEAVING

for Darcy

Dreams of Leaving was first shown on BBC TV in January 1980.
The cast included:

WILLIAM	Bill Nighy
ANDREW	Andrew Seear
STIEVEL	Johnny Shannon
COLIN	Charles Dance
AARON	Julian Littman
CAROLINE	Kate Nelligan
STONE	Tony Matthews
KEITH'S LAWYER	Raymond Brody
KEITH	Gary Holton
XAN	Mel Smith
AN OLDER JOURNALIST	David Ryall
MISS COLLINS	Annie Hayes
ROBERT	Hilton Macrae
MINISTER	Peter Williams
MRS ALEXANDER	Helen Lindsay
DOCTOR	George Raistrick
LAURA	Maria Harper
Photography	Mike Williams
Producer	David Rose
Director	David Hare

I. EXT. ENGLISH COUNTRYSIDE. DAY

*The English countryside. Green hills, cows, trees. Then suddenly,
without warning, rushing through frame, a British Rail Intercity train
hurtling along unseen rails. It passes. We look at the empty track.*
  Then the words: 'Dreams of Leaving'.
  Then WILLIAM's *voice:*
WILLIAM: (*Voice over*) I first came to London in 1971.

2. INT. TRAIN. DAY

An open carriage, every seat taken. WILLIAM *coming down the aisle
of the train looking for a seat. He is scruffily dressed in a corduroy suit
with a white mackintosh which he wears throughout the film. He has
one large suitcase and carries eight newspapers. He is from
Nottingham. He is twenty-four, tall, attractive, badly turned out.*
WILLIAM: (*Voice over*) Time of course has cemented things over,
  so this now seems like the inevitable course. But at the time I
  had no idea what I was doing. I didn't know if it was
  breakfast or lunch.

3. EXT. EARLHAM STREET. DAY

WILLIAM *coming out of the door of his new flat and walking along the
pavement. Behind him, the Victorian façade of a redbrick central
London block, in one of the small streets off Cambridge Circus. It has
a warehouse on the ground floor; then, above that, we see the arched
windows of a tiny group of small flats.*
WILLIAM: (*Voice over*) I pretty soon found a place where I could
  live and at the beginning girls were easy to meet : . .

4. INT. CINEMA. NIGHT

WILLIAM *sitting alone in the cinema. One seat away is an*
AMERICAN GIRL, *heavy with denim. She is big-boned, dark-haired,
about twenty-one, also sitting alone.*
WILLIAM: (*Voice over*) Perhaps the only time in my life that's
  been true.

(*An extract from the film he is watching:* Duel in the Sun. *Jennifer Jones runs to the cell door to plead for a stay in her father's execution.*)
I even picked a girl up at the cinema, something I wouldn't even contemplate now.

5. INT. WILLIAM'S ROOM. NIGHT

The room is very small and looks like a student's bedsitter. An old armchair, a bed, a messy roll-top desk. Little effort to decorate: some magazine pictures on the wall and a couple of prints. An old black-and-white television. WILLIAM *and the* AMERICAN GIRL *lying in bed together.*
AMERICAN GIRL: All right?
WILLIAM: What? (*Pause.*) Yes. Yes I'm fine.

6. INT. WILLIAM'S FLAT: KITCHEN. NIGHT

WILLIAM'S *view of the* AMERICAN GIRL'S *back as she stands talking at the stove wearing only a miniskirt and a feather boa round her neck. With one hand she is scrambling eggs, with the other she is drinking gin.* WILLIAM *sits at a small table by the wall. He looks subdued.*
WILLIAM: (*Voice over*) Everyone says Americans are obsessed with hygiene, but it never seemed to interest the ones I met.

7. EXT. FLEET STREET. DAY

A large newspaper office seen from the outside. A great black building. Then, once it's established, WILLIAM *running at high speed out the door to catch a passing bus.*
WILLIAM: (*Voice over*) I managed at last to get a job round the time I was living with someone called Angela, or thought I was, because she was never there . . .

8. INT. WILLIAM'S FLAT: STAIRS. NIGHT

WILLIAM *hastening up the brown-painted stairway to his flat.*
WILLIAM: (*Voice over*) It was six days before I realized she'd left me and another six before I could get over it.

9. INT. FLATS: ANDREW'S ROOM. NIGHT

The door of Andrew's room opening as WILLIAM *leans in from the corridor. It is identical to William's in shape, but it is tidy and painted white. Bookcase, scrubbed wooden table where* ANDREW *now sits working under an Anglepoise, his books and papers stacked around him. He is the same age as* WILLIAM, *very quiet and dry. A naturally grave and decent man.*

WILLIAM: Angela not here?

ANDREW: No.

10. INT. WILLIAM'S ROOM. NIGHT

WILLIAM *coming into his own room. He turns the light on and stands at the door. The eiderdown is on the floor, the clothes are all over.*

WILLIAM: (*Voice over*) Part of me knew she was with someone else and part of me wouldn't admit it because . . . no, let's stick to what I have to say.

11. INT. NEWSPAPER OFFICES. NIGHT

STIEVEL *in a huge open-plan office. At once the phone rings. At once he picks it up.*

STIEVEL: Night desk. (*Pause. He makes notes.*) Yeah. (*Pause.*) Yeah absolutely. Don't worry, Lonnie, the whole thing's in hand.

(WILLIAM *has arrived and is standing holding some grubby sheets of paper as* STIEVEL *puts the phone down and spikes his notes. He is about fifty, very casual in shirt sleeves, with very thick pebble glasses. Behind him the huge newsroom stretches away, now quiet. The pooling of the light makes it emptiness very beautiful.*)

WILLIAM: Somebody left me this stuff to go over.

STIEVEL: OK, sure, let me take a look. (*He takes the paper, looks at his watch.*) Did you get time off for supper?

(WILLIAM *shakes his head.* STIEVEL *reaches for the bottle of whisky on top of his desk.*)

Here. Help yourself. Have some of mine.

(WILLIAM *takes it and drinks as* STIEVEL *checks through the copy.* WILLIAM *looks across to the far entrance, some thirty feet*

139

away, where CAROLINE *and* AARON *are now standing. She is thin, dark-haired, good-looking, about twenty-four, smart and easy in boots and a loose dress, unmistakably from classless London; as it proves, Notting Hill. She is much taller than* AARON *who is only five foot, with long black hair, like a decadent schoolboy. He seems about eighteen, but is really twenty-five, and Cockney.* STIEVEL, *oblivious, checks through, emphasizing certain words.*)

Senior government ministers *assembled* . . . it was beer and *sandwiches* for lunch . . .

(WILLIAM *watches as, from his desk on the other side of the room,* COLIN *gets up to greet the strangers at the door.*)

COLIN: Ah, can I help you? Are you who I'm waiting for? (*He is in his mid-thirties, very posh, with squashed features and crinkly hair.*) My name is Colin. I write the gossip. (*He smiles.*) Don't worry, it's all right, I shan't gossip about you.

(AARON *has already taken something from his pocket and now palms it across to* COLIN.)

Are you going to tell me where it comes from?

AARON: No.

COLIN: OK.

AARON: I mean . . .

COLIN: No. Fair enough. (*He stands a moment.*) Well, look. All right? I hope you'll excuse me. I'd be grateful . . . I'll just take a look.

(*He goes and sits at the nearest desk, swings the Anglepoise round, unwraps the tinfoil and examines his small lump of hash.* STIEVEL's *voice meanwhile.*)

STIEVEL: Talks in *deadlock* . . . nation held to *ransom* . . . old women dying in the *street* . . .

(WILLIAM *watches as* CAROLINE *and* AARON *talk very quietly together as they wait, an odd pair.*)

AARON: You hungry?

(CAROLINE *nods.*)

Go and eat pasta?

CAROLINE: Yes I'd like to.

AARON: I'm very hot on clams. I really like clams.

(COLIN *gets up, as if at Sotheby's.*)

COLIN: This looks first rate. I have to thank you. It's such a bitch getting decent stuff around here. I don't suppose you have anything harder . . .

AARON: We have laughing gas. But only in cylinders.

COLIN: Yes. (*Pause.*) Well, perhaps not. Why don't I . . .

AARON: Pay?

> (COLIN *gestures to the door, as he gets out his wallet. But* CAROLINE *is staring straight across at* WILLIAM, *her gaze absolutely level at thirty feet. She stares.*)

COLIN: Are you coming . . .

CAROLINE: Caroline. (*Pause.*) Yes. I'm coming.

> (*But she still doesn't move. She just stands, staring at* WILLIAM, *and then suddenly turns lightly to* COLIN, *and they go.*)

> How do you choose who to persecute?

COLIN: What?

CAROLINE: On the column?

COLIN: Oh well . . . I mean . . .

> (WILLIAM's *view of their backs as they disappear through the distant door.*)

> I don't think we'd call what we do persecution. I've always believed the public has a right to know . . .

> (*They've gone.* WILLIAM *turns back.*)

WILLIAM: Well? What d'you think? D'you think I should cut it?

STIEVEL: It's fine. It's absolute rubbish. (*He smiles.*)

> Congratulations. You have the house style.

12. EXT. STREET. NIGHT

A single lamppost throwing its light through the London drizzle on to the pavement. WILLIAM *passing on his way home. A pause. We look at the empty street, then* WILLIAM's *voice.*

WILLIAM: (*Voice over*) From that day on things were never easy.

> Something had changed . . . for the rest of my life.

13. INT. WILLIAM'S ROOM. NIGHT

WILLIAM *sitting in the old armchair opposite* ANDREW *who is stretched out on the bed. They both have glasses of beer.* WILLIAM *has just answered the phone.*

WILLIAM: Meryl. God. Hey. Good to hear you. Yeah, I meant to.

> Well, how are you? (*He looks straight at* ANDREW.) Fact is it's ridiculous, I'm in bed with measles. Andrew leaves my

medicine outside the door. (*Pause.*) No . . . (*Pause.*) No, I
know . . . (*Pause.*) Well, you know I would like that. (*He has
picked up what is obviously her very intimate tone.*) Sure.
(*Pause.*) I know . . . (*Pause.*) That would be very good. (*He
laughs a little.*) Yeah well . . . yeah . . . yeah . . . lovely . . .
(*Pause.*) Look, why don't I send you my stuff in a bottle?
That would be something. Wouldn't it? D'you think?
(*Pause. The tone changes.*) No, no, I promise I was joking . . .
(*Pause.*) No, well sometimes I can't tell myself. (*Pause.*) Of
course. No, well look . . . (*Pause. Then very cold.*) I'll talk to
you, Meryl.
(*The phone being put down at the other end.* WILLIAM *holds the
receiver away from his ear, looks straight at* ANDREW.)
Shameless. (*Pause.*) Ugly. (*Pause. He laughs.*) Absurd.

14. EXT. EARLHAM STREET. NIGHT

*Seen from across the street, the lights in William's flat going out one by
one.*

WILLIAM: (*Voice over*) I thought I could begin to clear up the
    shambles, I had the idea of sorting out my life.

15. INT. GALLERY: PUBLIC ROOM. DAY

WILLIAM *standing alone in a white space. He has plastered down his
hair, put on a clean shirt and tie, gestured towards cleaning his
raincoat. He stands, notebook in hand. Then after a few seconds,*
CAROLINE *arrives, friendly, in a white blouse and full skirt.*

CAROLINE: Are you the journalist?

WILLIAM: Yeah I'm William Cofax. I rang you earlier. It's good
    of you to meet.

CAROLINE: You must tell me . . .

WILLIAM: I just want some background.

CAROLINE: Yes. I'm sure. Let me do what I can.

16. INT. GALLERY: PUBLIC ROOM. DAY

*They stroll together through the large white room. Behind them are
highly coloured abstracts on the wall. There is an empty desk, like a
receptionist's, at which* CAROLINE *works.*

CAROLINE: This is really just the façade of the gallery. This is
where anyone can come in off the street. We have the usual
changing exhibitions; they're regularly advertised, anyone
can come. (*She stops and looks round the whole room.*) It isn't
really the centre of the business. The real selling . . . well . . .
that goes on elsewhere.

17. INT. GALLERY: VIEWING ROOM. DAY

*The door being opened on a small room, formally laid out. It is heavily
curtained in velvet, artificially lit and no more than twelve foot square:
like a plush cell. At one end there is an easel, now empty. At the other
three chairs, that's all.*
CAROLINE: You see. In here. This is where it happens. This is
where they do nine-tenths of their trade.
(*She has moved into the room and stands by the easel.* WILLIAM
*stays near the door. She gestures at the easel, then at the chair
dead opposite it.*)
The customer sits down. He's alone with the painting. (*She
smiles slightly.*) Once he sits down it takes nerve to get up.

18. INT. GALLERY STORE. DAY

*The store: a large room lined with shelves and canvases which are all
stacked away on rails.* CAROLINE *and* WILLIAM *walk, picking their
way round the sculptures, which are lying around, labelled, on the
floor. The paintings are mostly hidden till you pull them out on rails.*
CAROLINE *and* WILLIAM *coming down the centre, talking.*
CAROLINE: These are the bins. Mostly they hold this stuff,
release it on the market at a certain rate. The idea is to
protect any artist they sell. Too much of an artist's work
comes available and you pretty soon find his price starts to
slide. (*She smiles.*) Who wants to pay top price for a Picasso
when there are twenty other Picassos for sale? (*She stops by
the racks.*) So we keep an eye on all the other outlets, buy
everything up and hold it in here. (*She points to a sculpture*
WILLIAM *is walking round.*) Moore. (*Another.*) Hepworth.
(*She pulls out a canvas on a long rail, disappearing behind it.*)
Mondrian.
(WILLIAM *pulls one out. She comes beside him to look at it.*)

That's a Rothko. (*She considers it a moment.*) They sort of
float in space.
(*We look at it.* CAROLINE's *voice meanwhile.*)
That's why the galleries prefer dead artists. They don't spoil
the market by turning out more.

19. INT. GALLERY STORE. DAY

Later. WILLIAM *pulls out the largest canvas of all. A man being sick
in the lavatory.*
WILLIAM: What sort of price do people charge for a Bacon?
CAROLINE: Well, it entirely depends on the size. When we can
    get hold of one we look in the price book, there's a charge per
    square foot; we take a tape measure, work it out like that.
WILLIAM: But that's . . .
CAROLINE: What?
WILLIAM: Doesn't quality come into it?
CAROLINE: Of course not. Why should it? That's not our job.
    (*She slides the Bacon back.*)
WILLIAM: But if Bacon painted a masterpiece, wouldn't they feel
    that they had to charge more?
CAROLINE: Good Lord no, what, hell, are you mad? (*She smiles.*)
    Then when he did a bad one, they'd have to charge less.

20. INT. GALLERY. DAY

*Later. They walk together along an open space, paintings all turned to
the wall.*
WILLIAM: Something about it . . . it's really amazing . . .
CAROLINE: It's just logical. It's a business, that's all.
    (*They walk. He looks around, lost for something to say.*)
    I can tell it must hurt your ethics. Ethics mean so much in
    Fleet Street, I know.
    (*They smile.*)
WILLIAM: All right.
CAROLINE: Well . . .
WILLIAM: Would you come to dinner?
    (*She stops, turns and looks at him.*)
CAROLINE: Why do you find it so hard to ask?

21. INT. GALLERY OFFICES. DAY

WILLIAM *standing uneasily in the corridor outside some smart offices in the gallery. He is waiting. The door is slightly ajar. Away to the back of the offices by a window is a languid, dark-haired man of about forty, with his feet on the desk, talking into a phone.*

STONE: I tell you what I'm thinking. Let's dump the Hockney. I
   don't see why we shouldn't. It's easy to unload. (*Pause.*)
   Two men. That's right. Having a shower. (*Pause.*) How
   should I know? Shampoo? Could be soap.
   (CAROLINE *passes across the room with a few letters in her hand.
   She stands in front of a desk which we cannot see, handing them
   across one by one.*)

CAROLINE: Can I leave you these? I'll be back in the morning . . .

STONE: Tell you what, I'll throw in the etchings, call it a series
   then you're away . . .

CAROLINE: This is for Stone when he's ready to sign. (*She hands
   the last one across.*) I'm going out.

SECRETARY'S VOICE: Are you going out with the journalist?
   (*A slight pause.*) Why don't you ask him if he's got a friend?
   (CAROLINE *smiles, not knowing she's observed, an absolutely
   private smile, and turns back across the room, moving out of shot.*
   STONE's *voice rising insistently at the back.*)

STONE: Our attitude is this: it's a figurative masterpiece and if he
   doesn't like it let him shit in his hat.

22. INT. GALLERY OFFICE. DAY

CAROLINE *coming out into the corridor, smiling, fresh.*

CAROLINE: Where we going, William?

WILLIAM: Oh what . . . well . . . I was thinking . . .
   (*They stand.*)
   Well, to be honest . . . I was hoping you'd say.

23. EXT. GALLERY. DAY

WILLIAM's *and* CAROLINE's *backs as they leave the gallery, talking together.*

WILLIAM: (*Voice over*) I realize now from the beginning . . . I was
   never myself when I was with her.

145

(His hand, just failing to touch her back, as they leave.)

24. INT. WILLIAM'S ROOM. NIGHT

WILLIAM *opening the door of the room. It has been transformed. The lights are already on. For the first time it is tidy and covered with greenery, hanging plants. He has arranged lamps and cushions and covers and books. A Matisse cut-out on the wall.* CAROLINE *stands at the door.*

CAROLINE: This is nice. This is really terrific. I don't know why you kept saying it was vile.

(She goes into the room. WILLIAM *closes the door.)*

WILLIAM: No, well . . . I suppose it was silly . . .

CAROLINE: It's so stupid. I've never understood it, men always say sorry, they say it all the time.

(She stands across the room in her coat. WILLIAM *looks up at her.)*

WILLIAM: I wonder . . . could I get you some brandy?

CAROLINE: What?

(She stares, as if not understanding him.)

WILLIAM: I have some brandy.

CAROLINE: Oh yes. OK. *(Pause.)*

WILLIAM: I'm really pleased you decided to come back with me.

CAROLINE: What?

WILLIAM: Just feel . . . *(Pause.)* . . . a good time.

(She looks straight across at him.)

CAROLINE: William, I want to make love to you.

WILLIAM: Yes. *(Pause.)* Yes, I know. *(He smiles.)* I'm a very lucky man.

(She is still staring at him. He gestures slightly towards the bed.) Why don't we . . .

(She moves away to the window.)

CAROLINE: Who do you have living next to you?

WILLIAM: Oh, Andrew. He's an Arabic freak. *(He goes to pour two glasses of brandy from a bottle.)* He's doing his thesis in this strange little writing. He sits in there, works at it, never looks up.

(She is looking out of the window.)

CAROLINE: He sounds really terrific.

WILLIAM: Yes, yes, he's nice. His work is his life. *(He hands her a*

146

glass of brandy.) Here. Here, I drink to your happiness.
(*She looks at him again, in the same way as before. A pause.*)

CAROLINE: William, let's get into bed.

(*He moves to the door and turns out one of the lights, leaving just a bedside light on. She stands quite still at the window, not moving.*)

WILLIAM: He can speak thirteen dialects. Arabic languages. There are that many you know.

(*The sound of* WILLIAM *undressing and getting into bed. We stay on her.*)

The thesis he's writing is all towards a dictionary; it's a dictionary of sixteenth-century Arabic slang. He is really prodigiously clever.

(WILLIAM *sitting in bed.*)

He is really . . . a very clever man.

(*There is a pause. Then she turns round and takes her coat off, then walks over and sits on the edge of the bed, with her back to him. She begins to undo her blouse, then pauses quite still.* WILLIAM *watching her back. She speaks quietly.*)

CAROLINE: I love more than anything to make love to strangers. It's the only time I forget who I am.

(*She turns round towards him and starts to undo the remaining buttons. The telephone rings. Her blouse held across her breasts with her hand. She smiles. She looks at him.*)

Well?

WILLIAM: What?

CAROLINE: Aren't you going to answer it?

(*He shakes his head slightly.*)

Shall I answer it?

WILLIAM: Sure. If you like.

(*She suddenly reaches right across him for the telephone which is on the table by the bed, still holding her blouse with her hand. She lie across him to answer.*)

CAROLINE: Yes? (*Pause.*) Yes? (*Pause.*) God. Hello, Nicholas.

WILLIAM: What? Who is it?

CAROLINE: No, it's fine, it's why I left this number . . . (*Pause.*) What? What for? Oh my god.

WILLIAM: Caroline, will you tell me what's happening . . .

CAROLINE: No, of course not, don't worry . . .

WILLIAM: What?

CAROLINE: No, no, it's fine, I can be right along . . . (*She is involuntarily doing up the buttons on her blouse with her spare hand.*) You hold on there, I can be there in ten minutes . . . (*Pause.*) Yeah, I should bloody well hope so. I'll see you in a minute, OK? (*She puts the phone down.*) Well, I mean, shit, what can you do about it? Who'd have a brother, that's all I can say.
(*She starts to get up and get dressed again.*)
WILLIAM: When did you leave this number?
CAROLINE: Driving under the influence of drink. (*She puts her coat on.*) Anyone who does that, they're just asking for trouble. (*She smiles.*) It should be a principle. Don't drive with long hair.
(*She is dressed. She turns and looks at* WILLIAM *with great kindness.*)
Listen, that was a really nice evening. You should be . . . (*Pause.*) Well, you're a very nice man.
(*She smiles, looking at him fondly all the time.*)
WILLIAM: Will you . . . can you try to come back later?
(*Pause.*)
CAROLINE: Yes, yes I'll try to. (*Pause.*) Yes. Yes, of course.

25. INT. WILLIAM'S ROOM/EXT. EARLHAM STREET. NIGHT

WILLIAM *at his window looking down to the street.* CAROLINE *hurrying along the pavement, her coat tightened against the wind.*
WILLIAM: (*Voice over*) I suppose I waited a week for her phone call. I wanted to call her, but I was too proud.

26. INT. NEWS OFFICE. DAY

Lunchtime in the newsroom. Just a few reporters working, most of the desks deserted. Tape machines, distant typewriters. WILLIAM *on the phone at his very messy desk.*
WILLIAM: Hello, Caroline. Yeah. Yeah, it's William. (*Pause.*) He got off? Good. That's very good news. (*Pause.*) You really did it? You gave the police money? Well, I was always told that would work . . . (*Pause.*) Yes – well I wondered . . . you know . . . about dinner . . . (*He smiles.*) Sure we've had dinner, we can have it again. (*Pause.*) You want me to offer

you a different sort of evening? Well, sure, if you tell me what sort of thing you'd like . . . (*Pause.*) Well, it's just easier, I hardly know you, I don't know what sort of evening to choose . . . (*Pause.*) No, I don't think . . . (*Pause.*) Well, what are you saying? (*Pause.*) I think it was good, it would be good again.
(*There is a long pause. He stands his pencil on the desk, lets it fall. Stands it up again, lets it fall. Then speaks very quietly.*)
Oh, well right, you have my number. (*Pause.*) Yeah, all right, see you. (*Pause.*) Talk to you soon.

27. INT. NEWS OFFICE. DAY

WILLIAM *standing at the agency teleprinter, staring down at the words as they chatter out. Then he rips the sheet out.*
WILLIAM: (*Voice over*) That was the point I should have abandoned it. People love chaos. I went on in.

28. INT. HOTEL: RECEPTION ROOM. NIGHT

A small, dapper LAWYER *in a pinstripe suit, very smart.*
LAWYER: This is Keith's first public interview since his highly publicized period in gaol. Keith wants to talk about the state of British prisons, and also tell you something of the future of the band.
(*A small, private reception room in one of London's grandest hotels. At one end there are microphones, at the other a bar. In between, forty members of the press, ranged out in rows.* KEITH *on a chair behind the microphones. Behind him, the other members of the band, who are extravagantly dressed.* KEITH *is intense, Cockney.*)
Keith . . .
(*He steps aside.*)
KEITH: Yeah, well right . . . I think most of you know something . . . how the stuff first got planted in my flat . . .
(WILLIAM, *just arrived, at the very back, in his white mackintosh, looking round.* KEITH's *voice meanwhile.*)
I don't want to go back over that story . . . I think most people know it pretty well . . . What I'd like to talk about is what happened afterwards . . . it's not easy . . . it's not

something to put into words. Basically the whole prison experience is one that's defeating and non-productive all round.

(WILLIAM *sitting down next to* XAN, *a fellow journalist of the same age.* XAN *has long black hair and a big nose. He wears an overcoat. They whisper.*)

WILLIAM: Xan . . .

XAN: Good to see you.

WILLIAM: Have I missed anything?

(XAN *shakes his head, still taking notes.*)

XAN: Only just begun.

(*We pick* KEITH *up in mid-sentence.*)

KEITH: . . . there are inquitous indignities of the system, comparable only to the position inside Soviet Russia . . .

(WILLIAM *nods quizzically at* XAN's *shorthand.*)

WILLIAM: Martyr to British Justice?

(XAN *shakes his head.*)

XAN: Cretin Let Out of Gaol.

29. INT. HOTEL: RECEPTION ROOM. NIGHT

Later. Chaos. A scrum of freeloaders round the bar. The room very noisy. Television cameras, flash floods. XAN *trying to get served,* WILLIAM *looking out across the room.*

XAN: You know, I mean frankly everyone knows it, British prisons are an absolute disgrace . . .

(WILLIAM *watches as a woman journalist is nervously introduced to the band who are standing in a small formidable group.*)

But I take that story back to my editor, he won't even look up to spit in my face. (*He turns, two whiskies in hand.*) Redbrick journalism, that's what he calls it.

WILLIAM: I know. (*He takes the drink.*) Thanks. (*He smiles.*) They hate our degrees. (*He drinks, watching the room all the time, his conversation automatic.*) And we only mention prisons when there's a rock star. We wouldn't write a word about what it's really like inside . . .

XAN: What's your interest? This isn't your story.

(CAROLINE's *face glimpsed for a second at the far end of the room, as she slips out the door.*)

WILLIAM: Somebody told me they had a good sound.

30. INT. HOTEL: CORRIDOR. NIGHT

The remains of the reception seen through double doors. The odd
waiter still passing in a white jacket, the last television crew packing
up. Through the doors XAN *and* WILLIAM *come out supporting an*
OLDER JOURNALIST *of about fifty-five, in a heavy brown coat. He is*
having trouble standing up.
XAN: Right.
WILLIAM: You got him?
XAN: Yeah. Yeah, I got him.
　　(*The* OLDER JOURNALIST *slips some way to the floor. As he*
　　does he holds up his notebook above his head.)
OLDER JOURNALIST: I got a good story.
XAN: Course you have, Mike.
OLDER JOURNALIST: I got the most sensational story.
XAN: Yes. Yes, of course. Keep moving your legs.
　　(*They have him upright.* WILLIAM *wraps him round* XAN's
　　shoulder, then hangs back as they begin to move down the
　　corridor.)
WILLIAM: Bye, Xan.
XAN: Bye, William.
　　(WILLIAM *watches as* XAN *leads the* OLDER JOURNALIST *off*
　　down the corridor.)
　　Come on, old friend. I'll find you a taxi. You'll soon be
　　better. (*He calls off into the distance.*) Taxi! *The Times*!

31. INT. HOTEL: CORRIDOR. NIGHT

A long corridor, thickly carpeted. A row of pastel doors. At the very
far end of the corridor WILLIAM *is standing in his mackintosh leaning*
in slightly, listening at a door as he knocks.
WILLIAM: Hello. Excuse me. (*He opens the door an inch, then calls*
　　in, his head still bowed.) I'm looking for Caroline. (*Pause.*)
　　Anybody seen her? (*Pause.*) Is Caroline there?

32. HOTEL: BEDROOM. NIGHT

A shaft of light from the corridor as WILLIAM *opens the door. The*

*light falls across a darkened room in which there are two double beds,
one with a couple lying together, in the other a single man. In between
the whole room is devastated: old meals, half-drunk bottles of bourbon
and champagne, drugs, pills, spilt glasses of water, clothes lying at
random, a colour television flickering noiselessly in the corner.*
WILLIAM *looks. Absolute silence.*

WILLIAM: Caroline? (*Pause.*) Caroline?

> (*His hand reaching down to pull back the sheet which covers the
> sleeping couple in the far bed. He draws it back slightly. The
> body of the girl, who is plainly not* CAROLINE, *doped out, inert.*
> WILLIAM's *face staring down at her, dispassionate, cool.*)
> Where are you hiding?
> (CAROLINE's *voice from the door.*)

CAROLINE: William . . .

> (*He turns.* CAROLINE *is standing at the door, the bathroom door
> open behind her. She is wearing just a shirt, but she looks
> absolutely fresh and clean.*)
> Hello.
> (*She looks down, then back across at him, with tenderness.*)
> I knew you'd come back.

33. INT. HOTEL: CORRIDOR. NIGHT

Back outside the room, WILLIAM *sitting, head in hands, on a
Regency banquette in the corner.* CAROLINE *in a patterned dress and
boots standing opposite.*

CAROLINE: Come on, William, I don't understand it. What's all
the grief? What have I done wrong? (*Pause.*) Why do you
think . . . you've barely spent an evening with me, why do
you think you're entitled to feel hurt? (*Pause.*) Listen, it's
none of your business. Whatever I do. I had to change jobs.
These are the people that I have to work with. Sometimes I
stay with them. Well, that's all right. (*Pause.*) I don't see
what difference that would make to our evening. (*She kneels
down opposite him.*) I really want to see you.
(*A long pause. Then he looks up.*)
Let's move it, OK?

34. INT. HOTEL: STAIRS. NIGHT

WILLIAM *and* CAROLINE *coming down the stairs together.*
CAROLINE *is laughing and shaking her head, very cheerful.*
CAROLINE: God, well William I can't believe it . . .
WILLIAM: Why didn't you call me?
CAROLINE: What did you say?
  (*They disappear round the corner. We just catch the last words as
  they've gone.*)
WILLIAM: Those people looked really ghastly.
CAROLINE: Yeah. I know. I never take drugs.

35. INT. HOTEL: STAIRS. NIGHT

Further down the stairs, CAROLINE *reaches out and lightly stops*
WILLIAM *who is walking ahead.*
CAROLINE: I'd like to take you . . . I'd like to show you
  something. I'm really pleased. I've done something good.

36. INT. BAND'S OFFICES. NIGHT

*A wall of what turns out to be the band's offices. A series of beautiful
black-and-white slides, projected. First, a bedroom; a man lying in the
bed, a woman with her naked back to us.*
CAROLINE: Here. Look. This is the series. They were taken in a
  brothel. These are my best.
  (*The shot held, then changed to a woman standing naked at a
  basin in an empty room.*)
  What do you think?
WILLIAM: Yes. They're terrific.
  (*A girl standing in a G-string next to a man looking into a
  mirror.*)
  I didn't know they had them.
CAROLINE: What, brothels? Of course.
  (*A group of women sitting together on the sofa in their dressing
  gowns.*)
  The band is going to use this lot as projections. Part of their
  stage show.
WILLIAM: Ah, right, I see.
  (*Another shot of the sofa.*)

153

CAROLINE: You mean you didn't know there were brothels in London?

WILLIAM: Somehow I thought . . . it's such a strange idea.

(*Closer on the sofa.*)

CAROLINE: You should go. They're wonderful places. I know the addresses, I could soon fix you up.

WILLIAM: Well, I would rather . . .

(*Another slide.*)

CAROLINE: I can't tell you the trouble I had with the women. Getting them all to come in at once. They're all freaked out, all over London. I had to hire a couple of taxis and go round and literally shake them out of bed.

(*A couple more go by, flicking on quicker, as if rejected.*)

I tell you, I wouldn't like to do it for a living. Organizing that lot.

(*A single whore on a sofa, holding her dressing gown open. She is naked underneath.*)

Can you imagine? With a woman photographer.

(*Another whore, close.*)

That was the best part. (*A long pause.*) When they agreed.

(*Then she turns the light on. She picks up a camera and takes a photograph of him, without moving from where she is sitting.*)

I'm a very, very good photographer. Didn't you think so? Aren't they very good?

(*She gets up to turn the main lights on in the room.* WILLIAM *stays sitting at a glass-topped desk watching her.*)

WILLIAM: What else is it the band has you doing for them?

CAROLINE: Helping. Being around.

(WILLIAM *smiles.*)

WILLIAM: Are the band pleased? Do they like the photographs?

(*She turns at the door.*)

CAROLINE: Good lord, William, I suppose I should ask.

37. INT. BAND'S OFFICES. NIGHT

WILLIAM *sitting now in the main secretary's office, which has smaller executive offices going off it. It is very smart in leather and glass, with photos of the band and posters of their tours on its walls.* CAROLINE *is going from room to room collecting paper plates, plastic forks, to go with the salt-beef sandwiches and coleslaw which are in greaseproof paper in front of* WILLIAM. *She talks as she goes.*

WILLIAM: Somebody told me you'd been sacked from the gallery.

CAROLINE: Yeah, I committed an error of taste. I ran off fifty-
three lithographs. That was three more than the gallery
knew. (*She shrugs in the light from a far room.*) I figured what
the hell? It's all a commodity. The market's rigged. What
difference does it make?
(*She smiles as she returns. She has champagne from the executive
fridge, which is crammed with bottles of it.*)
Of course the point is they like to do the rigging. Nobody
else. I'd broken the rules.

WILLIAM: Well in a way you were making a protest.
(*She stops in mid-action and looks at him.*)

CAROLINE: No, William. No. I was ripping them off.

38. INT. BAND'S OFFICES. NIGHT

Later. CAROLINE *sitting cross-legged on top of one of the desks, the
champagne beside her.* WILLIAM *drinking from a paper cup. Their
food gone.*

CAROLINE: I had a strange Russian sort of mother. She was
hysterical. She made no sense. (*Pause.*) When her family
came out of Russia, they lived for a while at the Savoy. All
I've been told is . . . they ate so disgustingly the management
insisted they lunch behind screens. That was really . . . when
it came down to it . . . that was really their great claim to
fame.
(*They smile.*)
I had no childhood; Russians don't understand it, they
expect you to be adults from the age of five. I had no father,
somewhere we'd lost him . . .

WILLIAM: What about your brother?
(*She looks at him. Impenetrable.*)

CAROLINE: My brother? He's fine.

39. INT. BAND'S OFFICES. NIGHT

*They stand in the doorway of the band's offices, opposite each other,
close. They are looking at one another. One light is on in the offices
beyond. The corridor is dark.*

WILLIAM: Caroline . . . I wonder . . . I'd like you to come home
    with me.
CAROLINE: Yes, well I shall. (*She smiles.*) I'm on my way.
    (*Pause.*) I'm afraid . . . I like it to be easy. I know it's unfair.
    It's a weakness of mine. (*Pause.*) If only you could look . . .
    as if it mattered less to you . . .
    (*She turns the light out. Darkness.*)
    If it just mattered less to you, then you'd be fine.

40. INT. WILLIAM'S ROOM. NIGHT

CAROLINE *in close-up, her hair down, her face on the bedcover. They
are lying sideways across the bed. We are very close.*
CAROLINE: You have that look. I really can't kiss you. When you
    have that look, it freezes me up.
WILLIAM: What sort of look?
CAROLINE: The look that says 'help me'. I'm sorry. I can't.

41. INT. WILLIAM'S ROOM. NIGHT

WILLIAM *is very angry. He is standing up, trying to hold it back.*
CAROLINE *sits silently in the corner, her legs tucked up under her,
deep in the armchair.*
WILLIAM: Caroline, come on, I mean, god this is stupid. How
    can you do this? This is just mad (*Pause.*) I mean for god's
    sake you said you'd come home with me. Then when you get
    here you simply freak out. I mean, come on, do you think
    about my feelings? I mean, Jesus Christ, will you give me a
    break?
    (*Pause. Then she speaks very quietly.*)
CAROLINE: I know. (*Pause.*) It's stupid. I ask too much of you.
    (*She looks at him, the same level look we have seen before.*)
    I'm very frightened. (*Pause*) I'm in love with you.

42. INT. WILLIAM'S ROOM. NIGHT

WILLIAM'*s face.* CAROLINE'*s face. The Matisse print above the bed.
Nothing moves.*
WILLIAM: (*Voice over.*) Oh god. Yes. That was Caroline. (*Pause.*)
    She was always ready. One more trick up her sleeve.

43. INT. WILLIAM'S ROOM. NIGHT

CAROLINE *rocking with grief and joy in* WILLIAM's *arms. The tears are pouring down her face. They hold each other tight.*

CAROLINE: Oh God Jesus William I love you. You're the only man who's ever been kind. You're the first friend . . . the first friend I've trusted. God how I love you.

    (*She takes his head in her hands and looks at him.*)

    You are my friend.

44. INT. WILLIAM'S ROOM. NIGHT

Their faces lying serenely together on the pillow, lit only by the street lights from outside. WILLIAM's *eyes are closed.* CAROLINE's *open. They lie still in the bed.*

CAROLINE: William. (*Pause.*) William. (*Pause.*) I'm ready for some cocoa.

    (*He makes a small move.*)

    You stay. I'll make it.

WILLIAM: Good. Good and strong.

    (CAROLINE *throws the cover back. She is fully dressed. She gets out of bed and goes to the door,* WILLIAM *watching.*)

    (*Voice over*) It was certainly something unusual.

    (*The door opening. The hall light coming on.*)

    But it wasn't something I'd see catching on.

45. INT. ANDREW'S ROOM. NIGHT

ANDREW *is sitting in bed, naked to the waist, reading a very large book,* WILLIAM *and* CAROLINE *come in.*

WILLIAM: Andrew, I'd like you to meet Caroline.

ANDREW: Hallo.

CAROLINE: How are you?

WILLIAM: Andrew. Caroline.

    (*They stand smiling a moment.*)

CAROLINE: I've been cooking. I've made enough for all of us.

ANDREW: Good. Terrific.

CAROLINE: Cocoa. Sausage. And eggs.

46. INT. ANDREW'S ROOM. NIGHT

The three of them feasting on sausages and fried eggs, drinking cocoa.
ANDREW *is still in bed.* CAROLINE *in a chair and* WILLIAM *at*
Andrew's work table. They are all smiling and talking, eating eagerly.

WILLIAM: I certainly remember that evening I was happy. It was
    certainly the wierdest night I've ever known.

ANDREW: I used to feel some sort of shame in a way.

CAROLINE: Why?

ANDREW: Just because it's odd to like anything so much.

CAROLINE: Why be ashamed?

WILLIAM: I think you're lucky.

ANDREW: Well, I admit I don't feel it any more.

WILLIAM: I think what you are is some sort of ideal. Andrew
    needs nothing. Just his work and that's all. I came in
    here . . .

ANDREW: Yes, well, we've heard this . . .

WILLIAM: A complete Indian dinner untouched on the floor. It
    had been there for thirty-six hours.

ANDREW: Bollocks.

WILLIAM: Yes well, sure. That's what you say.
    (*They smile.*)
    (*Voice over*) We sat round talking. It became very easy.
    (CAROLINE'*s face smiling as she watches the other two talking.*
    unaware.)
    We were always closest when someone else was there.

47. INT. ANDREW'S ROOM. NIGHT

WILLIAM *on his feet at the centre of the room, the others watching. We*
join in mid-speech.

WILLIAM: . . . Do you know what I think is the great sin of the
    world? Surely, it's caring what anyone else thinks. We ought
    to be able . . . my god, it should be easy . . . we ought to be
    sure enough just to be ourselves. (*He smiles round the room.*
    The others smile back. CAROLINE *looks down, like a mother*
    embarrassed by her too-brilliant child.)
    (*Voice over*) Yes, I remember. I was very happy. I was very
    flattered. I felt I was loved.

48. BLACK SCREEN

WILLIAM: (*Voice over*) So it began, that very strange summer . . .

49. EXT. STREET. NIGHT

Notting Hill. A London bus going by, WILLIAM *getting off as it moves, then walking down the road.*
WILLIAM: (*Voice over*) Caroline said the best of her life . . .

50. EXT. STREET. NIGHT

WILLIAM *standing on the pavement outside a terraced house in Notting Hill. He has just rung one of the eight bells.*
WILLIAM: (*Voice over*) I lost my judgment, I had no opinions . . .
   (*He steps back and looks up to the first floor window.*)
   Slowly . . . oddly . . .
   (*Standing at the window, a bearded young man wearing blue jeans, nothing else, gazing ahead.*)
   I lost my eyes.

51. INT. CHUEN CHENG KU. DAY

An enormous Cantonese restaurant in Wardour Street. CAROLINE *and* WILLIAM *standing together waiting to be seated.*
WILLIAM: (*Voice over*) It wasn't a question of actually deceiving
   me, she told me everything, that's what was strange.

52. INT. CHUEN CHENG KU. DAY

CAROLINE *sitting across the table from* WILLIAM. *Plain white cloth, the simplest china. They have a plate of fried dumplings which they dip in sauce with their chopsticks.*
CAROLINE: So I had to say to him, we had a good night together,
   why can't we leave it, why talk about love? (*She smiles.*)
   People seem to want to drag you down with them. Why can
   no one be content with a night? When it's good? (*She smiles.*)
   I don't know, William, I don't understand it . . . (*She reaches
   across for his hand.*) I'm very grateful I know you, that's all.

159

53. INT. CHUEN CHENG KU. DAY

CAROLINE *looking up as the* WAITER *brings a whole carp in chilli and black bean sauce. It is set down.*
WILLIAM: (*Voice over*) She used to talk to me as if I were impartial. Did she never notice she hurt me as well?

54. INT. NEWS OFFICE. DAY

At the very far entrance to the enormous room, CAROLINE *sitting down in a single chair, smiling up at an* OFFICE BOY.
CAROLINE: No, I'm fine thank you, I'll just wait here.
(*The* OFFICE BOY *passes frame, turns back uncertain.*)
Please don't disturb him. I'm actually fine.

53. INT. NEWS OFFICE. DAY

At the other end WILLIAM *is working at his desk. The whole room is at its busiest, phones ringing, copy going back and forth, people calling across desks.* WILLIAM *in shirt sleeves, a tie loosely round his neck, totally absorbed in a pile of cuttings.*
WILLIAM: (*Voice over*) Of all the odd things, the one that amazed me, she used to come and watch me, not tell me she was there.
(STIEVEL *calls across from his big desk in the corner.*)
STIEVEL: Hey, William, have you got British Leyland?
WILLIAM: Yeah, I have it. Just hold it a mo.
(XAN *comes by, dropping copy on his desk.*)
XAN: Your feature.
WILLIAM: Yes. Thanks. I'll do it. (*He looks up*). Just leave it under all the rest of that stuff.
(*He stands up, still totally absorbed, still reading and walks across the room.*)
(*Voice over*) She used to say afterwards she'd never desired anyone as much as she desired me when I didn't know.
(*He stops, pausing, as if he knew he was being watched. He turns back towards us. We see the chair, now vacated, and just behind it a glimpse of* CAROLINE's *coat as the door swings shut.*)

56. INT. WILLIAM'S ROOM. NIGHT

WILLIAM *and* CAROLINE *lying apart on the bed, he looking up to the ceiling, she curled foetally beside him. They are both fully clothed.*

WILLIAM: Please . . . (*Pause.*) Please. (*Pause.*) Couldn't you just try?

    (*Pause.*)

CAROLINE: William . . . I tell you . . . it's my experience . . .

    (*Pause.*) In these matters trying doesn't help.

57. INT. WILLIAM'S FLAT. NIGHT

WILLIAM *lying in the bed.* CAROLINE *sitting on the side of the bed, with a book.*

CAROLINE: This is a long one, all right?

    (WILLIAM *smiles as she turns back to read.*)

    'In Memory of W. B. Yeats'.

    (*Pause.*)

      He disappeared in the dead of winter:

      The brooks were frozen, the airports almost deserted,

      And snow disfigured the public statues . . .

    (WILLIAM'*s voice comes over her as she reads.*)

WILLIAM: (*Voice over*) Always implicit there was always the promise, if I held on, the moment would come . . .

58. INT. WILLIAM'S FLAT. NIGHT

CAROLINE *sitting in the armchair in dead of night, reading quietly, as* WILLIAM *sleeps. As if she is watching over him.*

WILLIAM: (*Voice over*) All I had to do was to keep my faith with her, keep on trusting her, then we'd be fine.

59. EXT. COUNCIL FLATS. DAY

WILLIAM *talking across a balcony to a* WOMAN *who is standing in the doorway of a council flat. She is wearing a silver catsuit.*

WILLIAM: (*Voice over*) I spent that summer as a general reporter, interviews, diary pieces, foot in the door . . .

    (*To the* WOMAN) Do you think your husband will ever come back to you?

(*The* WOMAN *smiles and begins to answer.*)
(*Voice over*) Then I ascended to features for a while.

60. EXT. STREET. DAY

*Outside the block of flats. A telephone box in the foreground of the
shot.* WILLIAM *coming out of the main entrance, seeming to ignore the
box.*
WILLIAM: (*Voice over*) Most of my time I spent avoiding
    coinboxes. Every coinbox became a sort of lure.

61. INT. TELEPHONE BOX. DAY

WILLIAM *putting tuppence in.*
WILLIAM: (*Voice over*) Whenever she answered I sensed her
    disappointment. Oh Christ . . .
    (WILLIAM *speaks with false cheerfulness.*)
    Hello.
    (*Voice over*) . . . He's helpless again.

62. INT. CAROLINE'S FLAT. NIGHT

Almost pitch darkness. Just the slightest streak of light falling across
CAROLINE'*s cheek. That is all you can see.* WILLIAM'*s voice on the
telephone to her.*
WILLIAM: Caroline . . . (*Pause.*) Caroline . . . (*Pause.*) I just had
    to ring you. It's awful. I'm sorry. I'm in trouble. You know
    . . .
    (*A pause. A slight movement from* CAROLINE.)
    I'm so desperate . . .
    (*Pause.*) I really can't tell you . . .
    (*Pause. He is beginning to cry at the other end.* CAROLINE'*s
    shape does not move.*)
    I'm just sorry . . . I need you. You know. (*A pause. He cries.*)
    I'm sorry, Caroline. Jesus. I'm sorry . . .
    (CAROLINE *does not move.*)
CAROLINE: It's all right. You must go back to bed.
    (*She reaches away out of frame. The phone being put down. Her
    face passing back across the light as she lies down. Silence.
    Darkness.*)

WILLIAM: (*Voice over*) I never understood why she wouldn't console me. I never understood it. I never shall.

63. INT. PHOTO LIBRARY. DAY

WILLIAM *standing at a filing cabinet in the photo and cuttings library. There is one complete wall of green filing cabinets, and at the back of the room there is a sloping glass roof. Morning light.* XAN *is coming through the door.*

WILLIAM: Hallo, Xan.

XAN: How are you?

WILLIAM: What are you up to?

XAN: Middle-class agony. A column of my own . . . (*He pulls open a filing-cabinet drawer.*) How inflation hits the middle class hardest. The editor feels it's a very good idea . . .
(WILLIAM *takes a file and moves away to a table to sit down.* XAN *takes a tracksuit which has somehow been left in the filing drawer and puts it on top of the cabinets without remark.*)
How the working class keep stealing their handbags. How they have to wait so long for a train . . .

WILLIAM: How the smell of curry drifts into their gardens?
(XAN *turns, file in hand.*)

XAN: No. Not quite. We're not going that far.
(*He comes to sit down opposite* WILLIAM *and starts turning the pages of the file.*)
We aim for a tone of modest self-righteousness. All decent people getting a bad deal. Always getting mugged at Valencia airport; how they can't even get a plumber any more. (*He has begun to copy out a clipping into his notebook.*)

WILLIAM: Why do we do it? It's all so dishonest. I've come to feel . . . (*Pause.*) No, I can't say.
(XAN *goes on writing without looking up.*)

XAN: I only write to claim the expenses. It's my expenses they should publish I feel. That's where my wizardry is fully extended. If I could write as I fiddle, I'd be Mencken, I'm sure.
(WILLIAM *is staring at him.*)

WILLIAM: I was talking to someone . . . she was saying if I felt as I do . . . the only honest thing would be to confront them.
(XAN *doesn't look up.*)

163

XAN: Yeah. Well remind me, I'd like to be there.

64. INT. NEWSPAPER OFFICES: CONFERENCE ROOM. DAY

Editorial conference. STIEVEL *sitting down at the head of the plastic-topped table in the undecorated room. Twelve journalists sitting down around the table, papers and newspapers in front of them, most of them reading, smoking and talking at once.* MISS COLLINS *passing round with feature lists.*

STIEVEL: Right everyone. Our morning conference. What do we have to set the world on its ear?
(MISS COLLINS *handing him his list.*)
MISS COLLINS: The Queen's in Moose-Jaw.
STIEVEL: Thank you, Janice. Right. Round the table. Do we have any more? (*As they being to go round the table, one by one, reading out their plans,* WILLIAM'*s voice over comes in.*)
WILLIAM: (*Voice over*) I see in retrospect everything I did then, everything I said was trying to please her.

65. INT. NEWSPAPER OFFICES: CONFERENCE ROOM. DAY

WILLIAM'*s turn.*
WILLIAM: Yes, well. I can talk about football, talk about film stars . . . probably shall. But I do wonder why we never spend a conference asking ourselves why we do this job at all.
(STIEVEL *looks up to* MISS COLLINS.)
STIEVEL: Can we have some more coffee?
XAN: Black.
STIEVEL: With sugar.
(WILLIAM *still staring down the table at* STIEVEL.)
WILLIAM: Why we go on every day producing something we know in our hearts to be poor.
(*Pause.*)
STIEVEL: Now look . . .
WILLIAM: Listen, I don't . . . I can't claim to be different. I'm just as guilty as anyone here. But I have got tired of living with the feeling that we all end up writing less well than we can. (*Pause.*) I came here, I'd worked in Wolverhampton . . . by no means, not a very good job. But at least there was no special pressure . . . you never felt you had to level

164

everything down. I mean at this paper we all promote the fiction of nothing very difficult for the people out there. The British public is assumed to be stupid, and in a way that suits us all fine. That's what we offer as our permanent excuse for not actually doing the job very well. (*Pause.*) Well, I can only tell you, I walk down Fleet Street, I look, I go into the bars. There you'll find . . . the retreat into alcohol . . . the smell of bad conscience heavy in the air. (*Pause.*) Why do journalists all become cynics? Is it really the things that they see? Isn't it more likely . . . the cause of their unhappiness . . . is something to do with a loss in themselves?
(*He looks round. Silence.*)
I dread a lifetime randomly producing something which we all distrust and despise. I dread the effects on my person of a lifetime given over to royalty and dogs. If we who work here can't believe in it, how the hell can the people out there?
(*A pause.* STIEVEL *looks at him.* WILLIAM *anticipates his non-existent reply.*)
All right. Yes. I know it. I'm sorry. (*Pause.*) Listen. Excuse me. I'm afraid I must go.

66. INT. NEWSPAPER OFFICES. DAY

A long tracking shot as WILLIAM *and* XAN *come through the newsroom.* XAN *exultant.* WILLIAM *grim.*

XAN: Hey, that was great. You really did it. I never thought you'd do it. That was really great.
(*He puts his arm round* WILLIAM *who doesn't stop.*)
That was terrific. You just laid it out there. (*He punches* WILLIAM *lightly on the arm.*)
Alcohol. Wow. Hit them where it hurts.
(XAN *disappears into the next office.* WILLIAM *goes on.*)
WILLIAM: (*Voice over*) I wasn't speaking to anyone present. I was ashamed. I was speaking to her.

67. INT. BAND'S OFFICES. NIGHT

The band's offices. Deserted except for CAROLINE *who is clearing up her desk, and* WILLIAM *who is sitting in a hard chair on the other side of the room.* CAROLINE *is extremely angry as she moves about the office.* WILLIAM *is miserable.*

CAROLINE: So what do you want? D'you want to be congratulated? Is that it? Come on, William, are you out of your mind?

WILLIAM: No, I'm not . . . all I'm saying is, well it sounds stupid . . . all I think is I may have done some good. (*He looks across at her.*) Well, look for Christ's sake, it's you who encouraged me, it's you who's always saying what an awful rag it is . . .

CAROLINE: Yes. Right. Good. So you told them. Why do you expect me to praise you as well?

(*He suddenly begins to whine.*)

WILLIAM: Come on, Caroline, I can't be expected to . . .

CAROLINE: You told me excited . . . expecting . . . why did you come in here with a smile on your face? (*She turns at the filing cabinet.*) I never understand it, you say you're independent. You say you're a person who will stand on his own. Yet whenever you do something virtuous, you seem to think you're entitled to come to me and collect some reward.

(*A pause. She is hysterical, on the verge of tears. She suddenly spits out her words with great violence.*)

Well, that sort of weakness disgusts me. Do what you have to. Be your own man.

(WILLIAM *looks at her sharply.*)

68. INT. ANDREW'S ROOM. NIGHT

A poker school. Andrew's table has been cleared and set in the middle of the room. The players are pooled under the Anglepoise. Everyone in shirt sleeves, smoking cigarettes, drinking very cold beer. The game is seriously played. WILLIAM, ANDREW, XAN *and* ROBERT, *a self-consciously good-looking blond young man of about twenty-five who smokes cheroots.* ANDREW *quietly turns his hand down.*

ANDREW: Fold.

(XAN, *already out, smiles slightly at him.*)

WILLIAM: Do I have it?

ROBERT: No. I'll raise you two bob.

WILLIAM: I'll cover that. Raise you again.

(*He pushes a pile of coins forward.* ROBERT *looks at it, then matches it.*)

ROBERT: See that. Raise you a pound.

WILLIAM: I'll see you.

> (ROBERT *turns his hand over*.)

ROBERT: Queens and sixes.

WILLIAM: Aces and fours. (*He smiles*.) Thanks very much.

> (WILLIAM *pulls the money towards him, then starts to shuffle.*
> ROBERT *lights a cheroot, then sits back, his hands behind his
> head*.)

ROBERT: Xan has been telling me about your life here.
Apparently you've been seeing an old friend of mine.

> (WILLIAM *smiles, carries on shuffling*.)

All I can hope is you handle her better. I don't know anyone
who held her for long.

> (WILLIAM *slides the pack across to* ANDREW.)

WILLIAM: Andrew, can you cut? (*Then he looks straight across at*
ROBERT.) She's been a good friend to me.

ROBERT: Oh yes I'm sure. She is. For a time. (*He smiles*.)
Everyone always used to say she was ruthless. But I never
minded. She was so good in bed.

> (WILLIAM *takes the cards back, absolutely cool. Then speaks
> very quietly*.)

WILLIAM: Well I don't know. Who can judge people? (*He looks
round*.) Why don't we play for a bit more this time?

69. INT. DANCE CENTRE. DAY

WILLIAM *coming up the stairs at the Dance Centre*.

WILLIAM: (*Voice over*) And so it was, later in the summer, she
disappeared completely. She couldn't be found. I think in all
she was gone for a fortnight. Eventually she called me. She'd
been on her own.

70. INT. DANCE CENTRE. DAY

CAROLINE *sitting on a chair in a leotard, her lunch of yoghurt beside
her. The other dancers moving across the room with the rehearsal
pianist to go out to their lunch, talking as they go.* WILLIAM *walking
into the room*.

WILLIAM: (*Voice over*) She was in training. She'd joined a small
dance troupe. Dance and drama. A mixture of the two.

> (CAROLINE *is talking*.)

167

CAROLINE: I'm really pleased. I'd forgotten the discipline.

WILLIAM: What happened to the last job?

CAROLINE: Oh, I don't know. (*She turns towards an unseen mirror as she replaces a grip in her hair.*) I was very hurt. Some work was rejected. I'd had enough. I wanted to go.

(WILLIAM *looks at her.*)

WILLIAM: I wish you'd rung me. I'd like to have helped you . . .

CAROLINE: Why would you help me? I'm absolutely fine.

71. INT. DANCE CENTRE. DAY

Four girls performing to some stark Debussy, played at the piano. A choreographer walking around the girls. WILLIAM *watching from the rail.*

WILLIAM: (*Voice over*) I don't have to tell you. She looked a great dancer.

(CAROLINE'*s face as she dances.*)

I was utterly frustrated. I put the knife in.

72. INT. CAROLINE'S FLAT. NIGHT

For the first time we see Caroline's home. A long oblong room, it gives the impression of being nine-tenths floor because of the lack of clutter, and the deeply stained shiny floorboards. Otherwise, there are some patterned hangings and a wall of books. CAROLINE *sitting on the floor,* WILLIAM *with his back to the mirror over the large fireplace.*

WILLIAM: You must forgive me. I came to tell you. I don't want to see you. I think we should stop. (*Pause.*) I don't know what role I'm meant to be serving. You never use me. You just want me there. (*Pause.*) If only you could make some movement towards me . . . (*Pause.*) Touch me. (*Pause.*) I crave it, I'm afraid.

73. INT. CAROLINE'S FLAT. NIGHT

CAROLINE'*s face as she turns away to light a cigarette.*

WILLIAM: (*Voice over*) It took a long time. It was mostly silence. Whatever I said, I couldn't make her fight.

74. INT. CAROLINE'S FLAT. NIGHT

CAROLINE *smoking a cigarette*, WILLIAM *in front of her.*

WILLIAM: Look, you don't know what people say of you. People say to me you're a cold-hearted bitch. Everyone hates you, they find it offensive . . . people resent it . . . the way you're so sure. There's something about it, it puts people's backs up . . .

CAROLINE: Well, thank you, yes, I must bear it in mind. (*She is quite level, absolutely without sarcasm.*)

WILLIAM: Don't you understand, don't you see what I'm saying, it's me who sticks up for you, it's me who stays loyal . . .

CAROLINE: Yes. Yes, I see. And you want a reward?

WILLIAM: No, I'm just saying . . .

CAROLINE: It must be very hard for you. (*Pause.*) Yes, it's unjust. (*Pause.*) One hell of a world.

75. INT. CAROLINE'S FLAT. NIGHT

WILLIAM *sitting silent on his chair.*

WILLIAM: (*Voice over*) I felt disappointed, it wasn't what I wanted, I'd come for hysterics and loss of control.

76. INT. CAROLINE'S FLAT. NIGHT

They stand opposite each other at the door jamb. The door is open to the landing beyond.

CAROLINE: Well, that's it. You better go now. (*She leans across and kisses his cheek.*) I never loved anyone . . . I only love you.

77. EXT. NOTTING HILL. NIGHT

The house seen from outside. Through the first-floor windows we watch CAROLINE *moving about, clearing up coffee cups, ashtrays, apparently impervious.*

WILLIAM: (*Voice over*) Well, there it was. I'd done what I came to. I started to watch her, but it came on to rain.

78. INT. ANDREW'S ROOM. NIGHT

WILLIAM *coming in, in his wet mackintosh.* ANDREW, *as ever, at work at his desk, the Anglepoise on. He looks up.*

WILLIAM: Andrew.

ANDREW: Hey. You look pretty gloomy.

WILLIAM: No. No, I'm not. I'm just whacked that's all.
(*He smiles, takes a book from his pocket, gives it to* ANDREW.)
I happened to see this. It's a first edition . . .

ANDREW: Browning. Terrific. Thanks very much.
(*He smiles at* WILLIAM, *still holding his pen.* WILLIAM *stands.*)

WILLIAM: Hey listen, I was wondering, can we go to a movie? There's one with Carol Lombard which I haven't seen . . .

ANDREW: Oh good, well yes, I mean I'd really like to. The problem is just . . . I've a friend coming round. (*Pause.*) Perhaps you would like to . . .

WILLIAM: No, no I wouldn't . . . (*Pause.*)

ANDREW: I met her last Thursday. We just got engaged. (*He smiles.*) I hope at least you'll hang on to meet her. She's very nice. She works in my field.

79. INT. WILLIAM'S ROOM. NIGHT

WILLIAM *coming in the door of his room. His earlier attempts at decency have now collapsed. The room looks like a pigsty again. The eiderdown is on the floor. He stands.*

WILLIAM: (*Voice over*) I could see the future. I was inconsolable. I felt I'd been challenged. And utterly failed.

80. INT. COMMONWEALTH HOUSE. DAY

WILLIAM *coming up a very grand staircase in the company of a large group of reporters.*

WILLIAM: (*Voice over*) I then remember little of what happened. I know I was listless, I was bored and depressed . . .

81. INT. COMMONWEALTH HOUSE. DAY

A big press conference. WILLIAM *on his feet in a packed room of journalists, notebook in hand.*

WILLIAM: Can the Minister tell us anything of the progress of the EEC negotiations, whether the question of agricultural subsidies is coming up for reconsideration and whether our future partners are going to be any less intransigent about the financial contribution the British are going to make once we're inside the Market?

(*A pinstriped* MINISTER *of about fifty begins to answer in the bray of his class.*)

MINISTER: Well, let me deal with that question in five parts. First let me say of all these inequities, they will be best dealt with when we are inside . . .

(WILLIAM *sitting down again.* STIEVEL *is sitting beside him, as* WILLIAM *sits* . . .)

WILLIAM: (*Voice over*) I suddenly found myself popular with Stievel. I have the clear feeling he knew.

(STIEVEL *leans across to whisper in his ear, then bursts out laughing, like a schoolboy.*)

He'd put down my outburst to an unhappy love life. Now she was gone, he seemed very cheered.

82. INT. ANDREW'S ROOM. NIGHT

The poker school. The same group in the same positions, except ROBERT *has gone and been replaced by another similar young man.* XAN *watching* WILLIAM *deal.*

XAN: Has anyone told you? Your friend Caroline. Apparently she's back with Robert again.

WILLIAM: No. (*Pause.*) Oh really? (*Pause.*) Well, I wish him well with her. (*Then he speaks very quietly.*) Let's hope he doesn't turn out to have needs.

83. EXT. STAGE DOOR. NIGHT

The stage door of a tatty West End theatre, along an alley. An ACTRESS *comes out and embraces* WILLIAM. *She is wearing a great deal of make-up.*

WILLIAM: (*Voice over*) I had a series of rather grim girlfriends, some of them, well, not particularly nice.

84. INT. WILLIAM'S FLAT STAIRCASE. NIGHT

WILLIAM *and the* ACTRESS *hastening up the brown-painted stairway to his flat.*
WILLIAM: (*Voice over*) I suppose the truth is I badly needed flattery . . .

85. INT. WILLIAM'S FLAT. NIGHT

The door closing as WILLIAM *and the* ACTRESS *go into the room.*
WILLIAM: (*Voice over*) Anyone who wanted me, I'd take them in.

86. INT. WILLIAM'S FLAT. NIGHT

Continuous. We hold on the closed door. There is a pause. Then the voice over continues.
WILLIAM: (*Voice over*) It was later in the autumn I started hearing rumours. Caroline had apparently been getting very thin. Then they stopped. Then I heard around Christmas, she'd been found alone in her room.

87. INT. CAROLINE'S FLAT. DAY

The pictures of the prostitutes and the brothel which have been printed as black-and-white photos, and left on Caroline's desk. WILLIAM *looking through them.*
WILLIAM: (*Voice over*) Apparently she'd sat there, she hadn't eaten. When they found her she weighed barely seven stone. (WILLIAM *standing alone in the now deserted flat.*)
I thought if I go it will only upset her. So I just gave the doctor a ring.

88. INT. ANDREW'S ROOM. NIGHT

The only difference is that at the other end of the table, under another Anglepoise, BARBRA, *a pale chubby blonde, now works as well.*
WILLIAM *sitting at the other side of the room.*
WILLIAM: Well, they're saying it's just undernourishment. She had some idea of living on her own. Apparently the worst is . . . it makes her hallucinate. (*Pause.*) They're not worried.

They just think she's thin.
(*Pause.*)
ANDREW: I suppose you don't know . . . does she ever ask for you?
WILLIAM: Yes, I should ask that. I should certainly find out.

89. INT. ANDREW'S ROOM. NIGHT

ANDREW *and* BARBRA *returning to their work as* WILLIAM *gets up and leaves the room, goes out into the corridor and into his own room.*
WILLIAM: (*Voice over*) I started ringing, I rang in often. I mean I always rang at least once a week.

90. INT. WILLIAM'S ROOM. NIGHT

WILLIAM *lying wide awake in bed at night.*
WILLIAM: (*Voice over*) She began to get better. She put some weight on. But it counted for nothing. She'd lost her mind.

92. INT. EARLS COURT FLAT. DAY

Caroline's mother, MRS ALEXANDER, *wearing black, sitting on an ornate gilded chair in a highly decorated but very seedy flat in Earls Court. There is a great deal of gilded furniture and mirrors and lamps which now look neglected and tatty.* MRS ALEXANDER *is fifty-five, elegant, taut, emotional.* WILLIAM *sits opposite, uneasy.*
MRS ALEXANDER: You are the boy. She spoke warmly of you. She was much in love. You were always the one.
(WILLIAM *looks down.*)
WILLIAM: Well . . .
MRS ALEXANDER: It's all right. There is no accusation. You did what you had to. You followed your heart.
(*They sit across the room from one another, the darkness coming down.*)
WILLIAM: (*Voice over*) Her mother turned out to be very, very stupid. I spent the evening listening to her talk . . .
MRS ALEXANDER: I can tell you must be experienced, you are so good-looking I'm sure you're pursued. Such looks. Do you find them a handicap? No, not a handicap. A blessing, I suppose.

92. INT. EARLS COURT FLAT. EVENING

MRS ALEXANDER *in mid-conversation, unceasing.*

MRS ALEXANDER: Of course now she's left me, I have no money,
I've relied on Caroline, I've no money of my own . . .

WILLIAM: (*Voice over*) All evening I listened, the talk flowed out
of her, nothing would stop it. A life of its own . . .

93. INT. EARLS COURT FLAT. EVENING

Later. The dark almost down. MRS ALEXANDER *well warmed to her
themes.*

MRS ALEXANDER: The blacks are now all over this
neighbourhood, those who aren't blacks are invariably Jews
. . . it's just no longer a place for decent people . . .
(*She continues.*)

WILLIAM: (*Voice over*) It all seemed pointless. What good could I
do?

94. EXT. SPRINGFIELD. DAY

*Ext. of Springfield Psychiatric Hospital. A splendid façade with an
industrial chimney, lawns in front.* WILLIAM *walking along the
drive.*

WILLIAM: (*Voice over*) Later that winter she transferred to
Springfield. I went to see her.

95. INT. HOSPITAL: LOUNGE. DAY

The lounge of one of the women's wards at Springfield. CAROLINE *in
a velvet T-shirt sitting on one of the armchairs, alone. There are a
number of chairs, a colour TV, some tables with games.*

WILLIAM:(*Voice over*) She was feeling very bad.

96. INT. HOSPITAL: LOUNGE. DAY

WILLIAM *sitting opposite* CAROLINE *in the otherwise deserted lounge.*

WILLIAM: I'm sorry. I feel . . . I let you down badly. I should
have seen you earlier. (*Pause.*) I had a feeling . . . I brought
you some papers. Here. There's something to read. (*Pause.*)

I hope you realize . . . how much we miss you. You must be quick, we need you back there.
(*He gets up and bends down to kiss her, a little patronizingly, on the forehead.*)

97. INT. HOSPITAL: CORRIDOR. DAY

The lounge seen from the corridor. We watch WILLIAM *and a* DOCTOR *walking towards us, talking as they come.*

WILLIAM: (*Voice over*) Of course I suppose if I have to be truthful, part of me admits to a feeling of relief . . .

DOCTOR: . . . long-term damage, it's too soon to say . . .

WILLIAM: (*Voice over*) I'd always believed the things that she told me, everything she'd said about how one should live.
(*He shakes hands at the door, smiling.*)
(*To the* DOCTOR.) Well, doctor, I must thank you.

DOCTOR: No, not at all. I'm delighted to help.
(*The two of them walk out of the frame which is now empty. We stare at the room beyond.*)

WILLIAM: (*Voice over*) Now it turned out . . . well I was grateful . . . that's what I felt. Thank God she was mad.
(*There is a pause. Then* CAROLINE *crosses from the hidden part of the room and with her back to us moves out of the door at the very far end of the room. Very fast fade.*)

98. BLACK SCREEN

Held for two seconds, then:

99. EXT. FLEET STREET. DAY

WILLIAM *walking along Fleet Street in the evening rush hour, one face among five hundred on the pavement. He is older.*

WILLIAM: (*Voice over*) Since that time I haven't done badly, I have a family, a very kind wife . . .

100. INT. WATERLOO STATION. EVENING

WILLIAM *getting on to a crowded commuter train at Waterloo, then reading his paper on the train.*

WILLIAM: (*Voice over*) The paper has been losing circulation, so of course we've all had to keep on our toes. That situation has been quite interesting . . . though most of the time I'm chained to a desk.

101. INT. HOUSE: HALL. NIGHT

WILLIAM *coming through the door of his house. A very pleasant cork-tiled, pine-furnished house full of plants and flowers. His children playing indoors as he comes.*
WILLIAM: (*Voice over*) Laura and I have had some very good times together . . . holidays, parties, evenings at home. Ben is much the most active of our children . . .
(*We see through to the kitchen where* LAURA *is preparing dinner. She is small and dark, very attractive in blue jeans.*)
Ellen, the youngest, was born a bit slow.

102. INT. KITCHEN. NIGHT

WILLIAM *pouring out gin and then tonic into two ice-filled glasses, taking them across to* LAURA *who is now at the stove. They are talking and smiling.*
WILLIAM: (*Voice over*) We've always tried to keep an open marriage. I mean I think a marriage is refreshed by affairs. I wouldn't necessarily recommend it to everyone, but if you can do it . . . and not go too far.

103. INT. SITTING ROOM. NIGHT

Later. Darker. WILLIAM *and* LAURA *sitting at opposite sides of the room, both quietly reading.*
WILLIAM: (*Voice over*) Obviously Caroline is much with me. I mean it's something I shan't ever forget. What I always took to be her self-confidence, now seems a way she had of hiding her fears.

104. INT. CHILD'S BEDROOM. NIGHT

BEN *fast asleep in his bunk. He is five. His face is serene on the pillow.*

WILLIAM: (*Voice over*) It breaks my heart that she couldn't reach
out to me. If I'd been wiser perhaps I would have known.
(WILLIAM's *face comes into frame as he reaches for the small
bedside light in front of* BEN. *The light goes out. Darkness.*)

105. INT. BEDROOM. NIGHT

WILLIAM *and* LAURA *sitting on opposite sides of the bed, undressing.
The warm light of a single bedside lamp.*
WILLIAM: (*Voice over*) If anyone now asks me what I feel about
these incidents, I can only tell you what I think for myself.
(*His wife's graceful body as she gets into bed.* WILLIAM *reaching
out to embrace her. Their faces as they kiss. A long pause. They
look at each other.*)
Our lives dismay us. We know no comfort. (*Pause.*) We have
dreams of leaving. Everyone I know.
(WILLIAM *turns away. The camera pulls out. The light is
suddenly turned out.*)